EVERY BUMP
COUNTS

HOW EVERYDAY ENCOUNTERS AND
RELATIONSHIPS CAN MAKE AN
ETERNAL IMPACT

BARBARA CRYMES WEST

HIGH BRIDGE BOOKS
HOUSTON

CONTENTS

INTRODUCTION

In this book, we will tackle the issue of how relationship is a foundational concept of leadership. Whether in the context of an organization or church, home or family, we all lead someone, and the principles of leadership are the same. What we do as leaders and as individuals revolves, first, around our relationships: the ways we grow them, the manner in which we nurture them, and where they lead us.

Do our relationships impact our leadership abilities? Can nurturing relationships change how we treat followers and how followers respond to our leadership efforts? And, finally, does it really matter?

In this book, we will go on a journey of discovery that has been an exciting adventure in my personal life. We will attempt to uncover some interesting nuggets along the way.

Where there is no leadership, there is chaos. Where there is no relationship, there is no effective leadership. Rather than a discussion that is wholly about the merits of different leadership styles, *Every Bump Counts: How Everyday Encounters and Relationships Can Make an Eternal Impact* will attempt to connect you to the process of becoming a person who can lead effectively and who God can use for His glory.

At the completion of this work, I hope that you will continue to think about the ideas presented and be moved to "make every bump count."

1

A Servant's Heart: The Least, the Last, and the Lost

The sun was shining, and I entered the office as usual, wishing I could have stayed home to enjoy the spring weather. I had just entered the reception office when I noticed that it felt as if something bad had happened. It reminded me of the atmosphere on the morning of September 11, 2001. My steps slowed as I took it all in. Sensing my concern, Janet broke the uncomfortable silence and said, "Hannah Osbain passed away last night." Immediately, tears came to my eyes as I processed this news.

Hannah was one of the Special Education students at the high school where I worked. Hannah had been a part of the school system since before I began working there. She was there every day and greeted everyone as she made her rounds with her one-on-one assistant, Pax. Hannah had suffered a very high fever as a young child and had not been the same since. In addition, Hannah had recently been diagnosed with Lou Gehrig's Disease. The diagnosis had been given so recently that her condition was not widely known. This fatal condition was ultimately what had taken her life the night before.

Hannah always had a smile for everyone. She could say "hi" and her name as well as some very basic sounds and words. She carried a basketball constantly and tossed it to her assistant while they walked through the hallways, greeting everyone every day.

Hannah's parents were a part of the church and the community. Her father, Randy, was a custodian for the school district as well.

Finally, after moving past the initial shock, I commented to Janet that, at last, Hannah was with Jesus and completely whole.

Janet replied, "Yes… Hannah had a servant's heart."

For many years since Janet's reply, I have contemplated what it means to have a *servant's heart*. I understood the truth of what Janet had said, but I had never considered what that really meant.

THE HOMECOMING

In 2000, as a foster parent, I received a nine-month-old baby from Child Protective Services (CPS) in my town. David came to me underweight, in size-3-month footed pajamas, and with a burn mark on his bottom. His footed pajamas were so small that he was unable to straighten his legs. My heart broke for this little guy who had already had such a tortured life, yet the broad smile on his face told a different story. I determined that, as long as he was in my home, I would address his issues, love him as my own, and attend to his deficits to the best of my ability. Within a month, David was walking. He had been to the pediatrician for his various ailments, and we were "loving him up."

Eight years separated David from my other two children. At the high school, I worked in the daycare center for students with babies. David went to school with me every day and rarely left my side. His burn healed, and he had various corrective surgeries over the next two years. For the next four years, David fought to catch up and struggled to overcome his deficits. Progress was slow.

As a single mother parenting three busy children, men from our church often took the boys on special errands, workdays, and involved them in various special events. Partly, the men were trying to bless me, but they were also filling the hole in the boys' lives as they were growing up without a father in the home. Unfortunately, none of my three children had a father figure, someone to call *Daddy*... someone with whom male parent bonding could occur. They had no male figure to model for them how boys become men and how young ladies should relate to men. David was eventually the only remaining child at home. The men's group continued to teach, nurture, and model godly behavior.

After having David as a foster child in my home for three years and jumping through the hoops to make him legally free for adoption, it happened! David became our own. He had a new birth certificate and a new middle and last name. He was officially mine.

Even after his adoption was complete, the men's group continued to invest in David. They taught him to cook so he could help at the monthly men's breakfasts. He was invited to several Northwest Men's Conference events and other enjoyable things through the years. These men— Foster, Dan, Dean, Peter, and Arthur—served David with servants' hearts. They taught David the importance of helping others, putting aside selfish desires, and exhibiting godly behavior.

Today, David is 16 years old. He still struggles in school, although not nearly as much as he once did. He no longer acts inappropriately in social situations, and he doesn't know a stranger. He loves fashion, and his is a social life. David isn't a perfect child... far from it. But David has a servant's heart. He volunteers to help at several community events every year, and as a junior in high school, he is ready to "letter" in community service.

David doesn't associate with only one group. As I like to say, he "cross-pollinates" his friendliness into other on-campus social groups. This year, David joined Link Crew, an organization on campus that helps incoming freshmen by taking them on tours of the campus, buying pizza for them, helping them to understand their class schedules, and befriending those who feel lost, least, and definitely last. Link Crew is an opportunity to build relationships. When David filled out his application for Link Crew, he asked me, "Mom, what makes me a good candidate for Link Crew?"

I replied, "Oh, that's an easy one. First of all, you have been in their shoes. You remember those first days and how important it was to you to have a Link Crew member assigned to you. Secondly, you are very friendly and don't know a stranger. And lastly, you model good student behavior every day."

This is my David with a servant's heart.

SERVANTHOOD

Putting others' needs before our own is sacrificial, humbling, time consuming, and often interrupts our own agendas. Jesus modeled servant leadership for us:

> For who is greater, the one who reclines at the table or the one who serves? Is it not the one who reclines at the table? But I am among you as the one who serves. (Luke 22:27)

Not only does God call us to servanthood, He also calls us to servanthood with right motives. We have been called to serve not for our glory but to glorify Him. Jesus also reminded the disciples in Matthew 23:11 that leaders must become servants.

Mother Teresa was a godly servant to the lost and dying in India. She served humanity for 70 years and remained Jesus' humble servant. The following quote by Mother Teresa paints a picture of a true servant's heart:

> I must be willing to give whatever it takes to do good to others. This requires that I be willing to give until it hurts. Otherwise, there is no true love in me, and I bring injustice, not peace, to those around me.[1]

If we consider Jesus as a servant, we must recognize His ultimate sacrifice. He laid down His life to conquer sin. The gravity of His sacrifice is that He had no sin, no guilt, and no debt. Through selflessness, He paid an unfathomable price. He counted the cost and still was willing to serve the sentence for your sin and my sin, for anyone who would believe.

God calls us to service and to give what we can willingly. Sometimes, it is a smile or a kind word. It could be more tangible and more expensive. Service and sacrifice come in all shapes and sizes.

Florence Nightingale, a child born to wealth in Victorian England, heard God's call on her life at 17 years old. History tells us that she served in the first field office in the Crimean War, revolutionized hospital methods, introduced life-saving nursing techniques, and started a school to train women to become nurses.[2] Although wounded soldiers adored her, she suffered disapproval from others most of the time because she didn't follow the contemporary social norms of that day. Women, especially those born into high society, were expected to marry and bear children, perpetuating the family bloodlines. She wrote,

> I am 30, the age at which Christ began His mission. Now no more childish things, no more vain things, no more love, no more marriage. Now, Lord, let me only think of Thy will.[3]

During her ministry, she became an advisor to kings, queens, and to the President of the United States while maintaining a servant's heart.

Nurse Nightingale nurtured a relationship with Mrs. Broomhead, the wife of a servant in her childhood home. Long after Florence left that home, she corresponded with

Mrs. Broomhead during her prolonged illness, encouraging her, praying for her as she endured her pain that God would give her peace and joy in the midst of her suffering. This service continued until Mrs. Broomhead's death over four years later.[4]

Florence Nightingale had a "caring and continuing relationship, even at a distance, with people of all stations in life, including her Mrs. Broomhead, the servant's wife."[5] Ms. Nightingale's desire to do God's will and serve from her heart led her to relieve the suffering of the least, the last, and the lost. She endured great sacrifice throughout her life and counted it joy for the Lord she served.

Whenever and however God calls us to serve, we are simply to be extensions of His love. He calls us into a relationship with Himself so that we might learn to live in relationship with others by loving them as He loves us and to impact lives for His glory.

SERVANT LEADERSHIP VIRTUES

As believers, we are called to serve those who we bump up against in our daily lives. Servant leadership, however, takes servanthood to another level. Servant leadership theory is a relatively new theory and one that has been closely compared to transformational leadership. Servant leadership has not been accepted as widely as more traditional leadership theories.

Transformational leadership focuses on the organization while servant leadership focuses on the follower. Transformational leaders strive to move followers to do more than is expected of them. Transformational leadership is about using *inspirational motivation,* encouraging followers to achieve more than is expected and reminding them of their importance to the organization; *intellectual stimulation,* lending support to followers as they develop ways in which their work can improve the organization; *individualized consideration,* supporting follower issues with specific directives or coaching in order to help them be fully actualized; and *idealized influence,* an emotional component that models behaviors that followers want to emulate.[6]

Although servant leadership theory has not been as widely accepted as other more traditional theories, there has been a paradigm shift in leadership theory in the past decade, presenting as a possible subset of a "new theoretical understanding of transformational leadership" based on Kuhn's approach.[7] Servant leaders seek first to serve rather than looking first at the organization's bottom line. While transformational leadership focuses on the organization, servant leadership focuses on the follower. This is where the two leadership styles part ways.

Servant leadership is based on virtue and builds on the internal characteristics of the leader, which ultimately leads one toward human excellence.[8] Dr. Patterson writes in *Servant Leadership Theory,*

> Servant leadership encompasses seven virtuous constructs, (a) agapao love, (b) humility, (c) altruism, (d) vision, (e) trust, (f) empowerment, and (g) service.[9]

Dr. Patterson goes on to say, "Trust is linked to integrity," and "trust is a building block for servant leaders."[10] Service is the heart of servant leadership theory.

It is the primary function and a critical element of leadership to serve first the needs and interests of others before self.[11] The behavior of a leader who strives to use servant leadership constructs can impact the organizational culture by modeling for his or her subordinates what service looks like and what it feels like when received.[12]

Effective leaders nurture and care about their followers' needs and listen to their concerns. They must share their goals, be willing to be vulnerable, and assist followers in growth. Essentially, servant leadership calls the leader to love his followers as Christ loves each of us. Everyone wants love, seeks love, deserves to be loved, and should be empowered by their leaders to extend love to others.

What Does Servant Leadership Look Like?

As discussed above, leaders who use the servant leadership style, first and foremost, put the needs of the followers not only before the needs of the organization but most assuredly before their own needs. If we consider how much time each of us spends at work, it is clear that it is in the best interest of the follower to be treated with respect and dignity. Followers who are fortunate enough to work for a servant leader and experience a "close-up view" of servant leadership virtues in their work life are more productive, have a higher level of trust for each other and authority, and are also invested in the success of the organization, which leads to a higher level of job satisfaction.[13]

As individuals, we go home to a family and move into our family leadership positions there. Being treated with love, humility, vision, trust, empowerment, and service in the work environment makes us better leaders at home.

Jesus told us, "A new command I give you: Love (agapao) one another. As I have loved you, so must you love one another" (John 13:34, NIV). First, notice that Jesus did not *ask* His disciples to love one another. There is no "please" or "it would be nice if" in the commandment. In that short sentence, He even tells us how to love one another: "As I [Jesus] have loved you." There is a clear emphasis on this command, one that leaders of organizations, families, churches, and other groups should heed. Winston says this in reference to the employee/follower relationship:

> There is a much greater sense from employees who stay with an employer because it is mutually beneficial on several levels: in physical terms, such as compensation; in mental terms, such as in a stimulating relationship; and in spiritual terms, such that the greater "self" is served and blessed by the involvement with the leader. This is the basis for love (agapao), to consider each employee/follower as a total person with needs, wants, and desires. Employees want to be considered for their brains and their hearts as well as their hands. The call of agapao love in the organization is to go far beyond seeing people as "hired hands," to seeing them as "hired hearts."[14]

I would be so bold as to imagine that, if we as leaders, in any and all aspects of our lives apply this same principle, we might see change all around us... change for the better. Imagine the impact consistent love for our spouses and children would make as we walk through the door after work. Consider the reaction of the casual contact we encounter as we "bump" shoulders with people at the grocery store while the line grows and frustration mounts. If we chose to love, respect, and give at every opportunity, we would be sending a clear and present message about our Savior, Jesus Christ. We would make every bump count and change lives in the process. Envision the impact on drivers during rush hour if you patiently let them into your lane during peak-hour traffic. Imagine what a smile might do for someone who lost his or her job that day.

Let's consider that each and every person we bump into each day has hurts and needs just like we do. Instead of thinking, "Oh, I'll never see this person again," what if we trained ourselves to think, "Next time I bump into that lady on the elevator, I'm going to give her an encouraging word." How different things could look with such a service-oriented perspective.

BUMPS

Allow me to take you back with me for a moment to November of 1999. A pink, squalling baby entered the world, born to a woman and man entrenched in drug addiction. Dependent on others for everything, this child's only means of fulfilling his needs was his voice. He needed food, shelter, and daily care. However, food and shelter were not enough to meet all of his needs.

Now, let's move forward to July 2000.

The phone call from CPS began a new life for this baby. No longer caught in the crossfire of domestic violence and abuse, love found David. The miraculously happy baby who entered my home that day, clothed in pajamas that kept his legs bent under him, only required love and nurturing to bloom into health. I bumped shoulders with David that day, and my life was changed. We began to build a relationship based on trust built from love. We began a journey that would take him from helpless infant to the vibrant boy he is today.

You see, David is one of the reasons why I believe that every bump, every encounter, and every smile is the foundation of relationship. Relationships matter. Just ask David.

---

[1] Very Best Quotes.

[2] Coakley, M.L., 1990.

[3] Ibid.

[4] Freeman & Glass, 2001.

[5] Ibid.

[6] Northouse, P., 2013, pp. 191-193.

[7] Patterson, K., 2003.

[8] Ibid.

[9] Ibid.

[10] Ibid., p. 8

[11] Farling et al., 1999, p. 64.

[12] Brown & Lord, 2001.

[13] Winston, 2002, p. 20.

[14] Ibid., p. 9

2

WHO YOU ARE

Why would You care about me? I'm so imperfect. I've made a mess of my life for years. You've taken me through the desert repeatedly, God, and I honestly don't particularly care to have sand in my shoes anymore. Please show me who You are and who I am. I'm sick of never learning the lesson and always waiting for the next desert experience.

This was my prayer and expression of my frustration due to a lack of growth in my spiritual life.

KNOCK, KNOCK

I grew up in the church and never considered not making it a part of my life. I gave my heart to the Lord at 12 years old because I felt it was time. I didn't experience the heartwarming emotional event that some people experience.

A knock on my door one day started a lifelong journey. The *knocker* asked me if I was saved, and after answering in the affirmative, he took it a step further. He asked, "How do you know you will go to Heaven when you die?"

I don't remember what I said next, but I shut the door and went into the kitchen to ask my mom how I could know that I was saved and going to Heaven when I died.

"Well, Barbara, it is a matter of faith."

"What do you mean?"

She simply replied, "When you ask Jesus to come into your heart, He does. Your part is believing that it's true. That is faith... believing that He is who He says He is and that He will do what he says He will."

Although simply put and sincerely offered, I struggled with similar concepts for many years to come.

Sand in My Shoes

As a single mother of two small children, I found my way to a church that was a wonderful place. It had programs for everything anyone could want. I began going to a singles' Bible study and served in the nursery on Sunday mornings.

During that season of my life, I was burdened with crisis after crisis. My life seemed to be connected by a short, single strand of peace between crises. I did a lot of crying and searching in those days, and I was blessed to find a friend to support me through them.

Karen was a sweet, caring young woman who had never married and specialized in "being sweet." I had the luxury of unburdening my heart to Karen frequently and being the recipient of her faithful, intercessory prayers. Throughout the year that I remained at that church, what stuck with me the most were Karen's words of encouragement to me. Literally, every time we spoke to each other, she would say, "Jesus loves you so much." Nice to hear, of course, but I wanted to experience what I saw in her eyes. I wanted to experience the realness and authenticity of the words she spoke. I wanted to *feel* those words rather than just hear them. I wish that I could tell you that I experienced that realness shortly thereafter, but I would be lying. You see, I had to get quite a bit more "sand in my shoes" during the next desert journey.

THE WOMB

It wasn't until about 10 years later that I began an adventure that changed me. It began by a commitment to read through my Bible in a year. When I had accomplished that, I did it again for another two years. For the next three years, I chose a different translation each year. Familiarity with the Word began to ignite a passion in me that drew me toward my Lord.

Soon, I found myself in a Bible study called *No Other Gods*, a book written by Kelly Minter. At first, I thought it was a study that wasn't particularly applicable to my life, but I was so wrong. In a matter of about two weeks, I became aware that God had led me into this specific study and that He had a plan. *No Other Gods* was just the beginning.

Without dwelling on every revelation or separate study or book that I went through, it is enough to say that my God was changing my heart. Scriptures began to spring from the pages.

Before I formed you in the womb I knew you,
and before you were born I consecrated you.
(Jer. 1:5)

Those words told me that, not only did He know me,
He also had a plan for me. He had made me in my
mother's womb, and my conception wasn't just
happenstance. He knew me way back then, but that wasn't
all.

For You formed my inward parts; You wove
me in my mother's womb... I am fearfully
and wonderfully made. (Psa. 139:13-14)

Are not two sparrows sold for a cent? And
yet not one of them will fall to the ground
apart from your Father. But the very hairs of
your head are all numbered. So do not fear;
you are more valuable than many sparrows.
(Matt. 10:29-31)

So, He knows the number of hairs on my head, and He
knows my name? Why would He bother? I mean, really?
He has a lot of other people He's looking after, all of whom
I was quite sure led more godly lives than I did.

I prayed for understanding, and I waited.

LADIES IN WAITING

The movement under my hand was relentless, especially
for my daughter as she carried my first grandbaby to term.
This baby, who we knew was a boy, was very active. As a

first-time grandma, I was very excited and anticipated Dreyson's arrival with every breath I took. I attended every obstetric appointment with my daughter, commiserated with her in the waiting, and kept the ginger ale coming as she moved into her third trimester. I hovered over Alison with fervor. A typical conversation with "the bump" went something like this:

> Hello in there. This is your Grandma. I love you, Dreyson. Remember that Grandma will always have cookies.

I know that sounds pretty goofy and even foolish, but that is who I am.

On one especially difficult day, we ended up in the labor and delivery department in an effort to check up on the baby. Alison hadn't felt much movement, and we were concerned. So, off we went. Hooked up to the monitors and giving Dreyson a chance to prove he was doing well, we listened to the heartbeat, thump-thumping into the room. We waited for what seemed like an inordinate amount of time. I couldn't be still another moment. What follows is not something I'm proud of, but nevertheless, I did it. I got down next to her, put my mouth on Alison's bare bump and began singing. I ran through my repertoire of songs from "Jesus Loves Me," "Oh, How He Loves You and Me," "This Little Light of Mine" and more, concluding with a rousing rendition of "I'll Fly Away."

A FOOL FOR LOVE

The things I do are a bit unconventional sometimes. My children remind me frequently that I'm different. But there is a point to my "foolishness." On that day in the hospital and every day, I wanted my grandbaby to know my voice. I wanted then and still do want with all of my heart to pursue a relationship with him. I was prepared to invest in his life from the moment we knew he was there until the day God would call me home.

Over the course of the next few years, I began to understand that, as my Abba Father, God wants me to know His voice. He wants to answer me when I call (Psa. 91:14-16; 116:1-2). He is invested in my life, and He desires that I invest in Him. Simply put, God wants a relationship with me, with you, and with all of His children. God never intended for us to walk through this life alone. He provided a mate for Adam in the Garden, and through relationship and the extension of His love to His creation, He continues to provide companionship, camaraderie, spousal intimacy, and counsel. He provides all of this through the love He freely gives and His endless pursuit of each of His children. It all begins with relationship. It can't be done any other way.

When we have our foundation in Christ and desire a deeper relationship with Him, even if all other relationships fall away as some do, we still will have a relationship with the Creator of the universe, our Abba Father. He is a "fool for love." He will do whatever it takes to pursue a relationship with you because being loved by Him is our purpose. So, you see, being foolish for the love of my grandbaby puts me in good company.

ENOUGH

If you are like me, your view of yourself can be quite disconcerting. I never felt worthy of God's attention toward me, His thoughts of me, or His love for me. Oh, in a general sense, I knew I was included with the masses. In other words, I accepted in a general sense scriptures that proclaim His love for His children but not in a personal, intentional, or specific way. I just couldn't internalize that kind of love.

> God is love. By this the love of God was manifested in us, that God has sent His only begotten Son into the world so that we might live through Him. In this is love, not that we loved God, but that *He loved us* and sent His Son to be the propitiation for our sins. Beloved, if *God so loved us*, we also ought to love one another. (1 John 4:8-11)

> The love of God has been poured out within our hearts through the Holy Spirit, who was given to us. (Rom. 5:5)

Over the course of time, I began to understand that my attitude was, in effect, a proclamation that the work that Jesus did on the cross wasn't enough. God's sacrifice of His Son, Jesus, and Jesus' spilled blood wasn't a big enough sacrifice to take care of my sin. Jesus' tortured last days weren't torture enough to redeem me. This realization humbled me. I suddenly knew that I had it all wrong.

In *The Divine Conspiracy*, Dallas Willard said,

He [God] matters because of what he brought and what he still brings to ordinary human beings, living their ordinary lives, and coping daily with their surroundings. He promises wholeness for their lives. In sharing our weakness he gives us strength and imparts through his companionship a life that has the quality of eternity... He comes where we are, and he brings us the life we hunger for. An early report reads, "Life was in Him, life that made sense of human existence" (John 1:4). To be the light of life, and to deliver God's life to women and men where they are and as they are, is the secret of the enduring relevance of Jesus.[1]

Indeed, He is enough! My selfish attitude had made it all about me when, in reality, it is about Who He is and what He did on the cross at Calvary. Jesus proclaimed the sufficiency of the godly sacrifice as enough when, from the cross to which he was nailed, he cried, "It is finished!"

SHINY AND NEW

On September 26, 2012, Dreyson made his phenomenal entry into our world. He arrived all shiny and new, a clean slate in my waiting arms. His life would never be less "written upon" than it was in that moment. Everything, both the good things and the bad things would leave their indelible marks. This child brought with him an enormous responsibility to those who would love him, care for him, and help him to grow up into the man of God he was intended to be.

It is the same thing with our Lord. When we come to a saving knowledge of His grace, we become all shiny and new. No sin. No sin debt. He lovingly and patiently waits for us to realize that, as His children, we need to snuggle up in His arms and let Him do His work in us. He wants to fulfill His plan and guide us as we walk in His will. He wants what is best for us. Our part is to seek an ever-deeper relationship with Him, our Abba Father.

> We were built to count, as water is made to run downhill. We are placed in a specific context to count in ways no one else does. This is our destiny.[2]

This is His will for us. Only through relationship with God can we be healed and whole. Only He can cover the indelible marks we gather through life. Love is the balm, the healing salve. Spread it liberally over your heart and mind.

---

[1] Willard, D., 1998.
[2] Ibid.

3

DARE TO LOVE HIM

RIGHTEOUSNESS

The subject of *righteousness* has always been confusing to me. What I know about righteousness was revealed to me quite recently. It was both profound and eye opening for me.

Scripture promises peace and good things to the righteous. God promises lovingkindness, knowledge, peace, good crops, and an anointing of joy in Psalm 36:10, Proverbs 11:8, Psalm 85:8, and Psalm 45:7, respectively. From Proverbs 10:2, we know that He speaks to the righteous, guides their paths, and delivers them from evil and death. There are countless promises of God for those who are righteous.

So, herein lies the rub for me. I am not righteous. I wrestled with this problem for many years, wondering how anyone can attain enough righteousness to be blessed by God in the ways He has promised. For years, I muddled through Scripture trying to reconcile the loneliness and isolation I felt because I didn't think I could qualify as righteous.

THE COST OF RIGHTEOUSNESS

My Aunt Suzanne once said to me, "It's not about what we do. It's about who He is and what He did."

I knew what she said was true, but I had never really internalized it. Then, one day in 2015, still muddling along and still seeking God in a fresh new way while very uncertain as to how that would happen, I read these words:

> For what does the Scripture say? "ABRAHAM BELIEVED GOD, AND IT WAS CREDITED TO HIM AS RIGHTEOUSNESS." (Rom. 4:3)

Could that be the qualifier I was seeking? I looked further and found Romans 1:1:

> For in it the righteousness of God is revealed from faith to faith; as it is written, "BUT THE RIGHTEOUS MAN SHALL LIVE BY FAITH."

Because of His death on the cross, Jesus redeemed us, paid the penalty for our sin, and became our righteousness. Wait... Let me say that another way. He bought the cloak of righteousness, and we—who, by faith, accept that redemption in the form of salvation—then qualify to wear Jesus' righteousness like a cloak! So, to boil that all down, I wear His righteousness because of Who He is and what He did! He paid the price for my sin and yours. Then, if we believe that, we get a new cloak. Those who believe get to go shopping on His dime. Now, I like that!

Relationships

Our purpose, in a general statement and yet foundational in our lives, is to have a relationship with the Creator of the universe. In this context, I'm not referring to your calling to serve on the mission field, to teach Sunday school, or to nurse patients back to health. The purpose I am describing is at the grassroots level of our being. In *Audacious*, Beth Moore describes what we would ask of God "if we only knew" what was available:

> If you only knew the gift I could give you and the ecstatic satisfaction of My Spirit within you...
>
> If you only knew what this relationship could be like and how boldly I love you and continually pursue you...
>
> If you only knew the transformative power of divine love received and reciprocated...
>
> ...Then you would ask Me, and I would give you.[1]

Did you catch that? "Divine love received and reciprocated..." That is relationship.

Circles of Influence

Each of us has a circle of influence, our immediate surroundings, where we each live our daily lives. I will discuss this deeper in a later chapter, but for now, I'd like each of us to examine our own circle.

The evidence of a lack of relationship is everywhere we look: beggars and outcasts, the homeless, the poor, other disenfranchised individuals, and anyone who is considered *different*.

From Biblical days, we can reflect on the leper and the woman with an issue of blood. I would bet dollars to donuts that each of them suffered from a lack of relationship in their lives. How? Let's take a closer look.

Lepers were required by law to holler out in a loud voice to anyone who came near them, "Unclean! Unclean!" Imagine the humiliation and loneliness.

Likewise, women of that day had a period of cleansing after childbirth that limited where they could go and who they could touch. Consider those we've all seen standing at the freeway off-ramp, appearing as though they have everything they own in their shopping cart. Consider those who suffer from mental-health issues and other maladies that cause them to lack social skills and decorum. I would venture to say that the relationships they form and maintain are not nearly as satisfying or abundant as the relationships of those who are not afflicted or those who don't endure "being different."

Relationships follow every one of us throughout our lives. As individuals, our relationships might look like friendships or family. They might take the shape of our favorite waitress or cashier. And likely, they take us to work and back. Relationships are—or, should be—nurtured and grown in the workplace as well as in our spiritual lives and in our neighborhoods. Without relationships, it is a lonely world.

DESIRE TO DO HIS WILL

Finally, let's consider how relationships influence our lives. Relationships involve giving and receiving. Some have a healthy balance of reciprocity while others don't. However, regardless of the type of relationship we have, all relationships come with rules. Take *honesty* as an example. Most personal and work relationships require a measure of honesty if they are to survive the test of time. Rules are boundaries that each person is required to stay within if the relationship is to flourish. For example, if a man wants to date a lady, the rules might be 1) pick her up on time, 2) be respectful of her "people," and perhaps, 3) don't call after 9:30 p.m. In this scenario, obeying the rules is a critical factor if he desires a second date.

God requires obedience from His children as well (Rom. 16:26). He desires a relationship with us, but He will not force His will on us.[2] He wants us to trust Him, and because of our love for Him, to be motivated to obey Him. By the shedding of His Son's blood, God sets each of us apart to be obedient to Jesus (1 Pet. 1:2), just as Jesus was obedient unto the cross (Phil. 2:8). Our obedience pleases God (Col. 3:20), and when we are obedient to Him, He favors us and blesses us (Exod. 19:5).

God set boundaries for us when He gave Moses the Ten Commandments. The "Big Ten" are the rules He commands us to live our lives by.

> "You shall love the Lord your God with all your heart, and with all your soul, and with all your mind." This is the great and foremost

commandment. The second is similar, "You shall love your neighbor as yourself." (Matt. 22:37-39)

If we love God, we will be obedient to Him. Following the previous scripture, we can then say that, "There is no true obedience to God without love of neighbor."[3]

Because you have in obedience to the truth purified your souls for a sincere love of the brethren, fervently love one another from the heart. (1 Pet. 1:22)

Obedience to the Father is our guiding light in loving others. In other words, as we love God, His commandments are walked out in our lives.

As I love God, I seek a deeper and more intimate relationship with Him. Through the process of seeking His face, I've come to hear Him more clearly and to trust Him more fully. I long to please Him. I cannot say this has been a purely pleasurable trip. There have definitely been tears shed and heart-wrenching decisions made at His urging. Sometimes, the tears have been the result of a walk through the valley of my fears. Other tears have been shed because He has so richly blessed me, once again causing me to be amazed by His lovingkindness, grace, and mercy toward me. He has shown me, in more ways than I can say, that He is there and has it all under control. I've had to remind myself countless times that, before anything comes to me, whether good or bad, it passed through the throne room of God. Nothing gets past my Savior and Provider.

In those times, He becomes my Comforter as we walk it out together in my life.

Walking in obedience to God, regardless of the difficulty, teaches us how to love others, lead others, and accept His love for us. The walk of obedience, hand in hand with our Abba Father, also reduces the number of miles on our desert journey and keeps the sand out of our shoes.

FOLLOWING THE LEADER

Followers follow trusted leaders. Again, this applies to organizations, groups, families, and individuals. Leaders who have proven their trustworthiness, integrity, accountability, honesty, and investment in their followers are easier to follow. At this point, I'm certain that I've made my position clear. These leadership qualities begin with relationship and build from that foundation. If we step back into the follower's shoes, we can identify with leaders who exhibit these qualities.

The same principle applies to the individual who pursues an ever-deeper relationship with the Savior. As we go deeper and experience His love and faithfulness, it becomes easier to follow. When God has "priors" for taking care of us, it becomes easier to allow Him to take us deeper with decreasing fear and increasing confidence in the end result.

FALLING

"If this doesn't work, our only recourse is amputation," the surgeon said.

A wave of emotion welled up within me as I tried to process the surgeon's words. I began to experience the typical "fight or flight" response as my adrenal glands rose to attention to help my body cope with the news. "Not again… Not again," I repeated inside my head. "I can't do this again."

I had just married my high-school sweetheart. That was in early November. By the end of November, my new husband complained of a sore spot on his leg that wouldn't go away. It was raining and dreary as he limped into the X-ray department where I worked to have films taken. Pulling the films out of the developer, I saw something that I had not ever seen before. With uneasiness, I took the films to the radiologist to be read.

He looked at me and said, "Whose films are these?"

I replied, "My husband's."

At home that evening, I fought the cold sweat that kept attacking me. In the late evening, I answered the phone.

My childhood friend, who worked in my department on swing shift said, "The report is back, and it says Sam has Osteogenic Sarcoma. Isn't that good news?"

As I dropped to my knees beside my bed, I replied, "It means he has bone cancer."

What followed in the days of my new marriage was a nightmare. Hospitalizations, operations, chemotherapy, hair loss, radiation therapy, sterility, and eventually metastatic lung cancer. Amputation was the course we endured as we attempted to save his life. We were both just 25 years old.

Déjà Vu

Nearly 40 years later and recently remarried, the doctor's words knocked the wind from my lungs. Within 10 days after a hip replacement, Jack had a raging infection. After countless surgeries to debride the infection, a wound vacuum (used to suck fluid out of non-healing open wounds 24 hours per day), and daily trips to the hospital for powerful IV antibiotics for two and a half years, Jack was referred to a plastic surgeon for wound closure.

We had checked into a downtown hotel on a Tuesday night and were settling into our room when the first call came.

"I'm sorry, Jack, but we have to cancel your surgery for tomorrow. Your recent MRI has detected Osteomyelitis. This will require an orthopedic surgeon to remove the diseased bone first. Then, the plastic surgeon will close the wound. We will call you when we have a new surgery date."

Let's fast-forward another month, another consult, and an extensive surgery to the post-operative appointment.

After the removal of several more inches of leg length, the surgeon dropped the bomb that echoed through our brains: "Possible amputation." I saw the color drain from my husband's face as he tried to process this critical piece of news.

How could I reassure him and say, "It will be okay, Honey"? I didn't know if it would be okay. I wanted to run away and not face the possibility of another high hip amputation. In fact, I began to fantasize that I was a sort of "Black Widow" who visited limb loss on those I married. Fear stood up tall and threatened to crush me... Crush us.

Months dragged by, peppered with more surgery, skin and muscle grafts, and a nearly six-month stay in a nursing home. I prayed. Oh, how I prayed. My prayers seemed to fall right back to me, unheard and unanswered. Friends, family, and church members supported us in prayer. Our lives were in a state of chaos.

And, remember David? He walked through it beside me, not knowing what to say, do, or think. Our world was upside down. My sky was falling.

PRAYER CHAIR

Done with begging and bargaining with God, my prayers began to sound like a belligerent teenager as I retreated to my Prayer Chair.

"What, God? What do You want me to do? I pray… I beg You for Jack's healing, but You don't answer me. In fact, things just get worse."

Daily, I retreated to my Prayer Chair out of desperation. Same result; different day. Slowly, the anger began to drain out of my broken heart. In the following days, I laid the ragged pieces of my heart out before the Lord. He had been there waiting, silently waiting for the noise in my head to quiet so I could hear Him.

An afternoon of agony stretched out before me. We had suffered setback after setback and were just struggling to keep our heads above water. With an anguished sigh that drained me of everything but my broken pieces, I heard it.

I cocked my ear to listen for it again. And, there it was: "Submit."

"What?"

Again, "Submit."

"To what?" I replied.

"To Me," He said.

Slowly, as the words of my Lord began to sink in, I began to feel a stirring in my heart. What could He mean? As I sat and thought about His simple words, I began to take my own inventory.

I knew Him.

I loved Him.

I knew He loved me.

And the list continued.

Next, I began to consider God's attributes. There were too many to list. He was my Father, my Protector, my Comforter, my Savior, and my Provider. As I meditated on the list, I heard His still, small voice again, dragging across the pieces of my ragged heart, a heart overcome by fears.

"Do you believe that I want what is best for both you and your husband?"

"Well, of course, I do. I think I do."

But could He possibly be saying that amputation of Jack's leg, above the hip, could be God's best?

The voice fluttered through my heart again. "If you believe Me, then trust Me and submit to Me."

ON MY KNEES

On my knees in that moment, the sky opened, and His love showed a light on my broken heart. I poured out the pieces of anger, resentment, despair, and self-pity and asked for His forgiveness. A great burden lifted from me that day. I began to accept that, indeed, Jack could lose his leg.

Weeks later, as I continued to trust and obey Him, God spoke to me again during my morning walk.

On a winter morning in December, I heard Him say, "Your obedience has made you whole."

Tears flowed as I did the "happy dance" right there in front of my neighbor's house. I would not be the same again. In that moment of rejoicing, I shook the sand from my shoes and walked on. I had dared to love Him.

---

[1] Kodell, J., 2013.
[2] Ibid.
[3] Ibid.

4

FOLLOW THE LEADER

Relationships are built on communication, whether direct or indirect, whether given or received. In personal and organizational environments, as leaders, honing our listening skills is critical to creating a culture that invites open communication. It is the responsibility of the leader to have his or her finger on the pulse of the followers at all times. An effective and respected leader knows when employees are troubled by work or personal issues. This knowledge is not known by being privy to the office "buzz" or from making frequent trips to the water cooler. It becomes known through time spent and effort exerted to build relationships with his or her staff.

Effective leaders nurture and care about their employees' needs, and they listen to their concerns. They must share goals, both personal and organizational. It is imperative that the leaders of today and tomorrow understand the cultures in which they do business with a keen awareness of cultural differences and sensitivity to the people they encounter along their journey.

It was "Pay Day Friday," and as was her custom, Mary was making rounds, delivering paychecks to each of her employees. Bethany had been under her supervision for a short time and was, as of yet, unaccustomed to this practice.

Hearing the knock on her office door, Bethany responded, "Come in."

The door opened, and Mary came in and handed Bethany's paycheck to her. Bethany accepted the check and thanked Mary.

Mary immediately turned and replied, "No, thank you!"

This was the first of many subsequent encounters that occurred every other Friday for the following three years.

Relationships are not static.[1]

> Relationships consist of cybernetic patterns
> of interaction in which individuals' words
> and actions affect the responses of others.[2]

Relationships are constantly changing as they are negotiated over time as a result of the feedback received from previous communications. Sometimes, the interaction—or, bump, as in bumping shoulders with someone—is a one-time event. Other bumps require growth and nurturing to become relationships. This is the responsibility of a leader, especially one who endeavors to practice servant leadership. Authenticity in dialogue fosters mutual satisfaction in communication and is an essential part of establishing trust in relationships. Relationships are built on individual behaviors within the relationship and are navigated over time.[3]

The process of developing relationships requires listening, individual interaction, and vulnerability. It can be compared to peeling the layers of an onion. As trust is built, individuals allow themselves to become more open and vulnerable. Individuals slowly allow people to penetrate their outer layers and become more personal or intimate in their interactions. Littlejohn and Foss refer to the dialogue that happens during this process as "shared moments."[4] Throughout the dialogue that takes place during the ongoing process of relationship cultivation, the tensions created from oppositional views are managed and made cohesive as the negotiation process moves forward. An interesting dynamic that occurs in the process of peeling the layers of the onion and nurturing a mutually beneficial relationship is something called *social exchange.*

SHARED MOMENTS

The premise behind social exchange is cost and reward value. Every decision has a cost and a reward. Each decision maker, whether follower or leader, must decide if the reward is greater than the cost and vice versa. For the leader, it might be something like, *Will loving my employees as Christ loves the church create a positive company culture?* or *Is the effort worth my time?*

The employee might think, *Is it safe to open up to my supervisor and let my walls down? I'm not sure that I want him to be in my personal business. Can I really trust that this is real and not some kind of control tactic that will end up hurting me later?*

During a spontaneous conversation with Mary as they traveled to a meeting together, the topic of Bethany's job interview process and content came up. Bethany mentioned that there was a question from her interview from months earlier that still "stumped" her.

Bethany stated the question: "Why shouldn't we hire you?"

Bethany asked Mary how she would answer the question if it had been posed to her during an interview. Mary thoughtfully and authentically answered the question. They experienced a shared moment.

Showing genuine concern for employees' issues and seeing them as individuals with strengths, weaknesses, skills, and vulnerabilities is vital to acknowledging their value and empowering them. Entrusting power to subordinates encourages them to do their best work. Leaders who demonstrate that they indeed value their employees create opportunities for staff to buy in to the company mission, engage in the work, and help co-create what the organization is trying to accomplish. Respected, valued, and empowered employees are creative, loyal, forward-thinking, service-oriented people.[5]

As Mary and Bethany communicated directly and indirectly, their relationship grew out of an established trust. Mary used listening skills and welcomed input from Bethany. Mary modeled servant leadership in several ways daily. When Bethany had a conflict with her young son being home alone for 30 minutes prior to Bethany's arrival, Mary negotiated a solution with Bethany that enabled Bethany to adjust her work schedule to be home when her son arrived. When Bethany lost her father and struggled in her grief, Mary shared comforting words from Scripture and their shared, personal beliefs. Bethany soaked up Mary's wisdom and considered it a gift.

When we look at Mary's leadership and Bethany's attitude and responses as a follower, we see the layers of the onion peeling away. Vulnerability increased, and trust grew with each subsequent social exchange. Social exchange led to shared moments that seemed to have begun with the mere delivery of a paycheck. This small interaction was the beginning of a relationship that was both individual and organizational.

Leaders who model this type of behavior will change the culture of their organizations one follower and one relationship at a time.[6] The organization will increase as each individual feels validated and supported. When genuine communication is spoken or acted out by the giver and received by the receiver, communication is complete.

COMMUNICATION

Communication is, without a doubt, an interesting topic... to say nothing of it's importance in relationships. Consider for a moment how we communicate. Communication is both direct and indirect. We speak words that we hope are delivered and received according to their intended meanings. Every day, we exchange dialogue with others in any and all settings in which we find ourselves. However, depending on our culture, ethnicity, age, economic station, or any number of factors, words can mean one thing to us and something totally different to another. Words can edify or tear down, convey seriousness or hilarity. Words can be twisted to mean something opposite from what we intended.

When people speak, they often insinuate
their intent indirectly rather than stating it as
a bald preposition. Examples include sexual
come-ons, veiled threats, polite requests, and
concealed bribes.[7]

We communicate with physical movements almost
every time we speak, even if a conversation is not face-to-
face with the other person. Think of a time when you were
having a conversation on the telephone and your hands
were waving wildly as you spoke. This is an example of
indirect communication. The hearer cannot use your
movements to interpret any meaning from your body
language.

With the advent of technology in today's world, we are
able to communicate in many more ways than before
internet technology. This "double-edged sword" allows us
to communicate much more today than ever before via
non-visual means. Text messages replace phone calls, and
email has virtually replaced the old-fashioned letter of my
childhood. We are fortunate to have technology at our
fingertips today as it enhances the speed at which we can
send and receive messages, easing the barriers of
geographic location. Meetings can be held without air
travel or consideration of time zones. However,
unfortunately for us, personal relationships can suffer as a
result of a lack of time spent together.

Indirect speech is inefficient, vulnerable to
being misunderstood, and seemingly
unnecessary.[8]

Extant literature has not been able as of yet to determine why people engage in indirect communication as opposed to "saying what they mean in the first place."[9] Indirect communication can either back up the message content or intent—that is, indirect communication can confirm its meaning, or it can confuse the receiver.

For example, depending on the circumstances, a wink can say to someone across the room, "I think you're cute" or even "Hello."

It can also say, "I have something in my eye" or "My contact lens just popped out."

As leaders and as individuals, it is important that our body language matches our oral messages. If someone says something with a smile, but the smile "doesn't reach their eyes," it can be confusing to the hearer. The intent of the message might be misconstrued as inauthentic or untrue. In *Overhearing the Gospel*, Fred Craddock pointed out that there is also responsibility in communication on the part of the listener.[10] Craddock communicated his high regard for Kierkegaard's work on direct and indirect communication by devoting an entire chapter to this topic. Kierkegaard did not believe in simply piling more information onto the listener but in creating a medium in which the listener had to engage and become a part of the information. Listeners must engage and listen for the meaning of the message. If the listener does not participate, the message is as "a breeze blowing by." The message is not taken in by its intended receiver, nor is it delivered. In such situations, communication is not complete.

For application, recall a time when you told a child or a spouse you would be late returning home. When you were late getting in, you found that your family was upset because they "were worried because you were late." Or, they might say they "didn't expect that you would be *that* late." The same communication mishaps occur in organizational and work settings as well. Without commonalities in communication, messages are difficult to complete. To be understood as a leader, we must learn who our followers are and how they consider the world. Then, we must craft our communication (knowledge sharing) to enhance the messages the followers receive and how they receive it.[11]

WORKPLACE COMMUNICATION

Communication is essential in all areas of our lives. Listening and understanding are two of the most important elements of communication.

> Listening is the attending, receiving, interpreting and responding to messages presented aurally.[12]

Much has been said about the art of listening. Sometimes, listening is indeed trying to hear what someone means rather than what they are saying. However, no person can read another's mind; so, as leaders, we must find ways in which to accomplish the end goal, communication. According to Nichols,

> Understanding and being understood is essential not only to reduce external and internal conflict but also to making ourselves more fully human.[13]

As essential as communication is in every aspect of our lives, so it is in the workplace. Understanding our coworkers as givers and receivers of information is important.

> By listening an individual gains clear insight
> into coworkers' and managers' concerns.
> Leaders create an empathetic climate through
> effective listening. Empathy is not sympathy;
> it is the capacity to relate to the experience
> and emotional foundation of another person.[14]

In the context of relationship building, I describe this type of listening and the pursuit of communication as "hearing their heart." Bradley and Jancewicz posit that the following six skills need to be exercised in what they refer to as "active listening":

- Paying attention
- Holding judgement
- Reflecting
- Clarifying
- Summarizing
- Sharing[15]

In an effort to complete the message, we must practice sending and receiving.

Traditionally, workplace communication has been viewed as something task-related that shares information and...

...develops quite naturally in organizations and... strongly influences production standards, performance norms, goals, interpretations of managerial and employee communication, and defines standards of effectiveness.[16]

The argument here is that communication is creative and can't be bound by communication rules. However, recent studies[17] have shown the importance of "positive social-emotional communication in overcoming communication problems (especially in creating work relationships)."[18]

In our turbulent global environment, we need organizational actors who recognize the importance of relationships, the potential diversity of message interpretation, and the ethical responsibilities that we each have as communicators who produce and reproduce the social world.[19]

Instead being used as a means of reducing overhead, the use of sick days, or the need for retraining, deliberate, skilled, and authentic communication can be used to benefit individuals. By increasing our understanding of one another and—as Bradley[20] proposed—recognizing the basic need for people to be understood, we can actually improve people's quality of life.[21] This is indeed in alignment with servant leadership virtues.

As a servant leader, Dr. Kathleen Patterson succinctly offers,

Servant leaders exhibit love in numerous ways. They show more care for the people than the organization's bottom line, are genuine and real without pretense, show appreciation, celebrate milestones, are sympathetic, listen actively, communicate, and are empathetic.[22]

Clearly, honoring our followers through efforts to understand them, listen to them, and communicate skillfully with them, we are building relationships that exemplify servant leadership. Again, I will say, "Relationships Matter"!

ACTING AS IF

As leaders, our actions must be consistent with what we communicate to our followers. Without congruence in all aspects of communication, there will be a lack of authenticity and trust. Without authenticity, communication breaks down, and relationships follow suit. As mentioned in previous chapters, relationships are important and legitimize the message presented.

If leaders fail in communication and relationship building, it can look like resistance. Resistance is a concern when change occurs. Resistance is a force to be reckoned with as it can sabotage change efforts and cause them to fail. We all experience change in our lives, for better or worse. For starters, we will look at organizational change.

Change resistance is a negative response that occurs for a variety of reasons.

[It] is a phenomenon that slows the change process by hindering its implementation and increasing costs.[23]

Fear is often at the root of resistance. Employees may fear job instability, economic changes, poor job outcomes, or simply not wanting to change the way things have always been done. As stated by Palmer,

Employees should be considered the cornerstones of any kind of organizational change because employee resistance is one of the biggest problems to contend with.[24]

Scholars agree that the duration of implementation and sustainability of planned change can take anywhere from six months[25] to two years.[26]

Trust is one of the biggest factors in reducing or mitigating change resistance. And as we've seen time and again, trust is built on relationship. Leaders who show genuine concern for employees, communicate frequently and authentically with followers, and engage in relationship building are in the best possible positions to ensure successful program implementation and sustained change.

Change Agents

Leaders must become change agents to guide followers through the process and help them avoid the pitfalls of change. Smooth transitions reduce stress and support the end goal of the change effort. Employees who respond to change positively can be recruited as champions to join the ranks of their coworkers and permeate the culture with what they view as positives to the change efforts. Effective leaders utilize champions to reach into places where they may not have access.

COMMUNICATION PLAN

Relationships built on trust and respect set the tone for input from key people in the organization. Empowerment of individuals occurs with inclusion in the process. Leaders empower employees when they invite ideas and are interactive with individuals.[27] Empowered employees will engage to solve problems and take ownership of the process.[28]

One way in which communication can be enhanced and increased is through the use of a communication plan. Encouraging employees to communicate and facilitating interaction between employees in all directions within the organization can be very beneficial. Providing employees with a space in which to connect gives them opportunities to engage in meaningful conversation, whether personally or organizationally related, and builds relationships. This practice allows them to transcend self and form "connectedness," which gives to them a sense of social responsibility at the organizational level and supports alignment of organizational values. Leaders who take an interest in what is happening in the lives of their followers are not only building relationships but are also practicing good stewardship of their positions. More importantly, they are practicing servant leadership behavior.

"I don't want to go. I like it just the way it is," hollered my son from his room.

My husband and I had been praying about changing churches and decided to visit a local community church with my parents. David had other ideas.

Our home church had a congregation of approximately 40 on a well-attended Sunday, all over the age of 40 years and the vast majority over 65. David was one of two teens, and there was no youth group provided. In recent months, I had begun to feel some unrest with our church that I resisted vehemently. I've always held with the view that "unless God directs, you'd better stay where you are and be faithful in your home church." I had seen too many people leave because of small disagreements or misunderstandings that they could not or would not work through. However, the nudging of God in my spirit was undeniable. I certainly tried to deny or ignore the nudging. This had been my home church for over 20 years. These people were my people and my support system. My children had never been anywhere else. And this was the rub for David. He was comfortable and didn't like the idea of something new. David didn't want change!

In order to keep David from totally digging in his heels, we approached "visiting Sunday" with little talk or fanfare. Sitting in church that morning, I prayed that it would be a positive experience for the whole family even if we made little progress. The music was upbeat with a worship team consisting of a lead guitar, bass guitar, drums, and a vocalist. The songs were familiar, and the technology used was up to date. David didn't have to be reminded to stand for the congregational singing.

On this particular Sunday morning, the high school seniors were recognized for their accomplishments, and the youth missions group was introduced and blessed as they were preparing to leave on a trip to California. A quick glance in David's direction told me that he wasn't hating it.

Later that day, David emerged from his bedroom, informing us that he discovered on Facebook that several of his friends and a few star atheletes from his high school attended the church we had visited. He had a look about him that began to tell a different story from his previous statement of resistance a few days prior. Seizing the opportunity, my daughter and I began to talk about how nice the service had been, that my grandson had not cried when left in the toddler room, and that there had been no battle to "shoosh" him during the long service. We commented on the music and both agreed that we had enjoyed the service.

"David, what did you think of church this morning?" I asked.

With a tiny, uplifted curve to his mouth, he replied, "It was okay."

David was being resistant to change. He didn't want change, and from his perspective, there was no need to discuss it further. He had subtly positioned himself to resist change to the best of his ability. Even though the possibility of change was good for the overall order, he would have no part of it. In this case, my grandson had been a champion for change. He had, for the first time, willingly gone to Sunday School and found it to be a good experience. His family had led the change plan and acted as change agents by offering information regarding the change. Supporting communication efforts with his friends, of course, had been the deciding factor. David had found meaningfulness and connectedness and had experienced a transcendance beyond self.

All the pieces fell together when we heard him say, "Church was okay."

---

[1] Littlejohn & Foss, 2011.
[2] Ibid.
[3] Ibid.
[4] Ibid.
[5] Winston, B.E., 2002.
[6] Patterson, K.,2003.
[7] Pinker et al., 2008.
[8] Ibid.
[9] Ibid.
[10] Craddock, F.B., 2002.
[11] International Listening Association, 2008.
[12] International Listening Association, 2008.
[13] Nichols, R.G. 1980.
[14] Bradley & Jancewicz, n.d.
[15] Ibid.
[16] Keyton et al., 2013.
[17] Barkse, 2009; Pullin, 2010.
[18] Keyton et al., 2013.
[19] Mumby & Stohl, 1996.
[20] Bradley & Jancewicz, n.d.
[21] Mumby & Stohl, 1996.
[22] Patterson, K., 2003.
[23] Christensen, M., 2014.
[24] Saruhan, N., 2014.
[25] Monnolla & Woton, 2015.
[26] Trybus, M., 2011.
[27] Kelley, D.A., 2014.
[28] Green, D.D., 2011.

5

THE CALL

Why are we here? What is our purpose in this life? These are age-old questions that have led many people and generations to begin a journey to "find themselves." I don't pretend to know the answers to these questions, but I hope to add some insight into what has come to be applicable in my life. Maybe I can share a little bit or a piece of understanding that will help you.

In 1966, Dionne Warwick sang a song written by Burt Bacharach and Hal David titled, "Alfie." This song, although I'm sure it began and was marketed as a secular number, has some relevant lyrics for this discussion.

> What's it all about, Alfie
> Is it just for the moment we live
> What's it all about when you sort it out, Alfie
> Are we meant to take more than we give
> Or are we meant to be kind
> And if only fools are kind, Alfie
> Then I guess it's wise to be cruel
> And if life belongs only to the strong, Alfie
> What will you lend on an old golden rule

As sure as I believe there's a heaven above,
    Alfie
I know there's something much more
Something even non-believers can believe in
I believe in love, Alfie
Without true love we just exist, Alfie
Until you find the love you've missed you're
    nothing, Alfie
When you walk let your heart lead the way
And you'll find love any day, Alfie, Alfie

It appears that Alfie was being asked the same questions individuals are being asked today.

At the risk of sounding preachy, let's go back in history to *Genesis*. Throughout Chapter 1, we see God creating the earth, the heavens, and the seas. Then, with His omnipotent hand, He got a little "artsy" and began the brushstrokes in vivid watercolor that brought plant life and animal life into being. And He thought it was all good.

But He wasn't finished yet. Oh, no… far from it. He changed mediums again and began sculpting from the dirt a man who looked like Himself but was not Him. At this time, a heavenly drum roll must have been heard as He stooped down and began the first-ever CPR. He breathed His breath into the man, and Adam became a living being. I'm not sure how the celebration looked on that day, but quite possibly, God created a spectacular "star-show" that set the heavens afire with what today would be described as the best fireworks display ever.

Why the blast of fireworks in the sky, you wonder? Why all the "hoop-la"? Well, because the first earthly relationship had begun. And in the words of my Heavenly

Father, "It was *good!*" This relationship was modeled after the relationship God had with the Son and the Holy Sprit before the Creation of the universe. You see, He wanted for man what He was experiencing in Heaven. He was hooked on man from that first breath. It was love at first sight!

As the fireworks died down, we see God planting and showing Adam how do make the soil work for him. Gardening and Animal Husbandry 101 had begun. God's vision was for man to have dominion over all He had created, that it would feed him and ensure sustainability on Earth. He was calling Adam to be a master gardener in the spectacular garden He called Eden. The name, Eden, comes from the Greek term for "park land" from which the word "paradise" is taken. God created Paradise as a place to fellowship with man.[1] Are you getting the picture?

After all this "goodness," God and Adam sat back and watched the first parade. Each creature followed the next in the walk past God and Adam while names were assigned. When I think about the "name line," I am awed by the creative abilities of Adam. Fresh out of the dirt, he must have had an extraordinarily creative mind to pull off that assignment. But, at the end of the day, God still had not found a suitable companion for Adam. And in that moment, God applied the first anesthesia and the first surgery of the universe. From Adam, God formed woman and gave her life as well.

Throughout the rest of Holy Scripture, from *Genesis* to "maps," God makes reference to relationships. He gave us instructions to serve, love, and honor others. What I find interesting is that—while instructing us on how to cleave, love, honor, obey, and serve others—His instructions began with applying those same instructions to our relationship with Him. Our foundation is God. He calls us to love Him, obey Him, seek Him, and grow in relationship with Him.

THE CIRCLE: WHO'S IN AND WHO'S NOT

"No matter what I do, it's not enough. I can't do enough… be perfect enough. I'm just never enough. I don't understand why my efforts aren't helping my marriage," Carol cried as she wiped her eyes and nose and added the tissue to the growing pile beside her.

Wendy posed a question, "Who is in the Circle?"

"What circle? What do you mean?" questioned Carol.

Extending a fresh box of tissue to Carol, Wendy replied, "If your marriage is illustrated by a circle, who is in it?" Wendy continued, "The Marriage Circle contains two people. If you look at your marriage, how many people do you see in the circle?"

Through a new onslaught of tears, Carol replied, "Just one. It's just me, I'm all alone."

"So, you can see that, in a relationship, both people must be present and participating. If one person steps out of the circle, the remaining person is alone. The relationship cannot exist with one person. It takes both," offered Wendy.

And so it is with our relationship with God. There is one difference, and an amazing difference it is. When other relationships fail—and, they *will* fail—our relationship with the Triune God will never fail. God *never* steps out of the circle! Why then did God create us as He did and teach us how to be in relationship with one another?

Our calling is to love God and others. *Others* may include church families, social circles, our individual families, and even our work families. Each of these individuals that we touch are impacted by what we say, how we conduct ourselves, how we treat others, and who we are. God created us and taught us how to be in relationship because, according to God's economy, relationships are foundational. They make the world go around. He calls us to "make every bump count" because "relationships matter."

DIFFERENT CALLINGS

On a more macro level, each of us has more than one calling. If we are married, we are called to love our spouse and to nurture and sustain that union. If we are parents, we are called to love, protect, teach, and nurture our children. As employees, we are called to do our jobs to the best of our ability with intent to be an asset to our employer. All of these aspects of our callings are about relationships and how we grow them and sustain them.

---

[1] Church of the Great God, 2016.

6

INDESCRIBABLE, UNFORGETTABLE, UNDENIABLE, INESCAPABLE

When considered through our human thought capability and language systems, God is indescribable. Who can describe the colors of the sunrise? Even our most-accomplished poets and most-beloved psalmists cannot do justice to the colors that grace our sky with the blush of each new day. As humans, we often resort to descriptions along the lines of "awesome," "amazing," "incredible," and "indescribable."

UNFORGETTABLE

Bear with me as I bring another old song to our attention. Written by Irving Gordon and made popular in 1951 by the great Nat King Cole, "Unforgettable" was undoubtedly written as a love song but clearly draws parallels to the Creator of everything. The song's orginal working title was "Uncomparable" and eventually changed to "Unforgettable." For our purposes, either title would suffice, but let's take a look at the words:

Unforgettable
That's what you are,
Unforgettable
Tho' near or far.
Like a song of love that clings to me,
How the thought of you does things to me.
Never before
Has someone been more...
Unforgettable
In every way,
And forever more
That's how you'll stay.
That's why, Darling, it's incredible
That someone so unforgettable
Thinks that I am
Unforgettable, too.
Unforgettable
In every way,
And forever more
That's how you'll stay.
That's why, Darling, it's incredible
That someone so unforgettable
Thinks that I am
Unforgettable, too

I declare those lyrics with the substitution of a few "darlings" for a few "Abbas" and a well-placed "and" in the line that says, "Tho' near [and] far," we are left with a song that describes the unforgettable love of the Father for His children. In this context, the words still fall short of an accurate description of God's indescribable unforgettable-ness.

Undeniable

God is undeniably everywhere we are and everywhere we are not. When we first saw a newborn baby entering the world, we were speechless and probably muttered something profound (or not so profound) like, "He is so perfect," or "She is so beautiful." Neither description did that baby justice, but they were the only words we could come up with in that moment, that moment when divine meets mortal, and the heavens rejoice. In those most-amazing and indescribable moments, God is undeniably present. There is no other explanation for such a miracle.

In another sense, let's consider the hermit crab. A homeless creature without a shell, it has no protection from predators, so it seeks an abandoned shell in which to hide and set up housekeeping. This is an example from nature that is indicative of an undeniable God. Who could have thought that plan up? Certainly, not you or I. You may be thinking, "Well, many will give the credit for such a unique system to Mother Nature." With a resounding, "Hogwash," I am convinced from the *Guidebook of Yesterday, Today, and Tomorrow*—otherwise known as the *Holy Bible*—that God created all systems that keep the stars in place and the waters within their boundaries. He arranged the tides and the creatures that live within our ecosystem to support the life that He created to live within it. The Psalmist, David, describes the power of God's voice in Psalm 29:

> The voice of the Lord is upon the waters; the
> God of glory thunders, the Lord is over many
> waters. The voice of the Lord is powerful, the

voice of the Lord is majestic. The voice of the Lord breaks the cedars; yes, the Lord breaks in pieces the cedars of Lebanon. He makes Lebanon skip like a calf, and Sirion like a young wild ox. The voice of the Lord hews out flames of fire. The voice of the Lord shakes the wilderness; the Lord shakes the wilderness of Kadesh. The voice of the Lord makes the deer to calve and strips the forests bare; and in His temple everything says, "Glory!"

In these descriptive verses, the Psalmist never even gets into a description of the power of God's hand or the power He used in *Genesis* when creating the world or in *Exodus* when He parted the Red Sea. He merely writes of the power of God's *voice*. He reminds us that, when God speaks something, it happens. He said it, so we must believe it. Without the power of Almighty God, we would not be here or anywhere to question it. Yes. He is that *big*.

David, the Psalmist, proclaims,

> The earth is the Lord's, and all it contains, the world, and those who dwell in it. For He has founded it upon the seas and established it upon the rivers. (Psa. 24:1-3)

God simply did not forget *anything*, not even the hermit crab, and He created *everything*. He is undeniably inescapable.

INESCAPABLE

In *The Divine Conspiracy*, Dallas Willard offers these words:
God is right here with us to look after us. And his presence is precisely what the word heaven or, more accurately, the heavens in plural, conveys in the biblial record as well as through much of Christian history. The Old Testament experience of God is one of the direct presence of God's person, knowledge, and power to those who trust and serve him. Nothing—no human being or institution, no time, no space, no spiritual being, no event—stands between God and those who trust him. The "heavens" are always there with you no matter what, and the "first heaven," in biblical terms, is precisely the atmosphere or air that surrounds your body.[1]

ANGELS ALL AROUND

My first awareness as I struggled to the surface of consciousness, fighting through the fog of anesthesia, was a trip I didn't relish and still don't to this day. "Waking up" is always confusing, and in those moments when surroundings still don't make sense, there is a sense of having no control. Not pleasant, in my opinion.

Facing a necesssary but elective surgery had me scared. I was concerned as with any surgery, with waking from anesthesia as smart as when I went to sleep. This surgery was the worst because I was single with two very young children who depended on me. I thought and prayed fervently about whether or not this surgery was the right thing to do. Unable to gain a sense of peace for the impending surgery, I called upon a trusted friend. In addtion to a compassionate ear, she prayed for me. She asked God to give me peace and safety, and she prayed that God would send a legion of angels to watch over me during surgery and bring me through anesthesia "as smart as I had been before it." Although I still struggled a bit, I chose to believe for God's blessing and moved forward with the operation.

Lying in recovery, finally fully awake, I began to recall a dream I had during the operation. In the "dream," I saw my body on the operating table with surgeons on both sides. Surgical nurses were attending the surgeon, giving him the various instruments he asked for and applying suction as needed. The operating suite was crowded, very crowded. And then, I noticed that it was full of angels. These were winged beings, clothed in white robes, standing shoulder to shoulder with every person in the room. As the doctors huddled over my body and peered into the incision, so did the angels. There was absolutely no unoccupied space in the room because it was filled to capacity, yet the surgeons and nurses were able to move about freely despite how crowded it was. The medical personnel were oblivious to the heavenly beings beside and around them. There was a sense of calm and peace that filled me as I watched the surgery.

And then, it hit me. People don't dream during surgery. Suddenly, I realized that God was confirming His answer to my friend's prayer. He had sent a legion of angels to the operating room that day to watch over me, just as my friend had asked. I knew that I knew the truth and reality of what I had just seen. I had been blessed with a living example of how deeply God loved me and cared about the outcome of that surgery. That day, God filled all the spaces around me, and as Dallas Willard described, "[He] was in the atmosphere [and the] air that surrounded my body."

My God and your God, the God of the universe, is inescapable, and His love for His children is indescribable, undeniable, and unforgettable.

> For in Him we live, and move, and have our being. (Acts 17:28)

---

[1] Willard, D., 1997.

7

Working It Out

Vocation

Within the scope of our calling and on a more macro level, we all have a vocation. As we serve God through our calling, we serve our neighbors through our vocation. Gene Edward Veith Jr. calls this the doctrine of vocation.[1] Although perfectly capable of taking care of people through miracles and divine acts, God most often chooses to care for us through what the world refers to as "the economy" but what theologically is the interaction of vocations.[2]

An example of this concept is our food. When I buy a loaf of bread, a farmer has grown the wheat, a mill has prepared the flour, and a shipping company has transported the flour to the baker who bakes it and sells it to me. I have been served through the vocations of the farmer, miller, truck driver, and baker's vocations. When I make a sandwich for someone else from the bread I bought, and on and on, I serve through my vocation as a food preparer.[3] This is God's economy and an illustration of the doctrine of vocation.

> In God's earthly kindom… Christians have
> different callings, and their complex
> relationships with each other become
> occasions to live out the love of God.[4]

Once again, we arrive at relationship.

"I'm sorry, but we've chosen another applicant. You seem over-qualified. Perhaps you could apply for something else?"

These were the endless messages I heard from the voices on the telephone. After relocating to another state and leaving a job I loved, I was desperate and motivated to find a job in the economically depressed area which I now called home. I had never been out of work and was determined that I wouldn't be for very much longer.

Eight months passed while I searched the market. Resumés, cover letters, references, want ads, and phone calls consumed my days for hours at a time. Looking for a job *was* my job. During that time, I volunteered for several non-profit organzations to make good use of my time and make connections that would help to grow my network. I had never had trouble landing a job and couldn't understand why I was now. People encouraged me and were supportive of my efforts, but nothing changed—at least, on the job front. In the background of my life, however, God was certainly at work.

I had searched the internet for months, occassionaly landing on the local college website in search of work. I even began looking at programs that might be of interest to me, but heard myself say on more than one occasion, "You don't need another degree. You need a job." Months flew by and still nothing. I prayed for guidance, interviewed, and begged God to hear my cry, yet I heard nothing.

In late July of 2012, I was still surfing the internet when I noticed a program at the local college that I hadn't seen before. I clicked deeper into the site and realized that the community college was offering a Bachelor's degree in management. I was intrigued. Could a bachelor's degree open doors of opportunity that had been closed in the past months? I felt a quickening in my spirit. Suddenly, I was aware that God was directing me to check out the program. Three weeks later, I was enrolled in the management cohort and on my way to a bachelor's degree, a dream that I never thought would be fulfilled. No longer silent, God had spoken.

Throwing myself into the undergraduate work, I studied hard, applied myself, and sucked up every morsel of information I could. As graduation drew near, I began to feel a restlessness in my spirit and began again to petition the Lord for guidance. I didn't know what I was supposed to do, but I began to feel called to continue my education and complete a graduate program in leadership. Back to the computer I went to research the possibilities. I had almost made up my mind to enroll in one of the colleges advertised on TV when an internet ad surfaced for Regent University. I had not considered finishing at a Christian college but decided to check into it. What I found there changed my life.

After a few phone calls, an application, an essay, and a transfer of credits one month later, I was an online student enrolled in Organizational Leadership at Regent University in Virginia. I was amazed at what God had done and where He was leading me. The blessings I reaped as I put one foot in front of the other through the graduate program were too many to count. From the moment I opened the first syllabus until the final assignment submission, I knew that I knew the God of the universe had heard my prayer and was guiding me on my journey.

At Regent, I had the support of phenomenal staff and students and the wisdom and teaching of many exceptional professors. I enjoyed exposure to global issues, and the courses provided excellent content, context, critical thinking skills, and Biblical application.

Over the two years of graduate studies, I learned not only about organizational leadership and Biblical principles but also grew to understand servanthood and what my responsibilities as a Christian are regarding my calling and vocation.

God led me and continues to lead me toward His plan for my life. It is a walk of faith every day. I have bumped shoulders with countless people as a result, and I have learned beyond all else that everything we do, everything we are called to, and everyone we meet as we move through this life is another bump. We might not see the significance of the bump, and we might not see the impact soon or ever, but we can be assured that every bump counts because relationships matter.

THE WORKPLACE

In previous chapters, we have discussed servant leadership and organizational behavior as well as how both individuals and organizations operate in the context of servant leadership virtues, communication, and relationships. A concept that is gaining more and more momentum in organizational studies is the concept of worldview and spirituality in the workplace.

WORLDVIEW

A combination of how we see the world and our philosophy of life is our *worldview*. Another way to explain worldview might be to compare it to a lens through which we view the world around us. The experiences we have from birth until the present have written on the slate of who we are, shaping and molding our thoughts and changing how we view the world.

For a Christian, the experience of rebirth has an impact on his or her worldview, but the conversion experience is not the same for everyone. If a person comes from an atheistic worldview, at conversion, not only does the person experience a saving knowledge of the grace of God but also suddenly acknowledges the very existence of God as Creator and Savior. If a person already believes there is a god or even one true God who created the universe, he or she will now know beyond doubt, based on faith, that he or she will live with God in eternity. The Christ-centered worldview is not static but is ever-changing as we experience life and grow as we are transformed into His likeness.

C. S. Lewis described his conversion as a process. Previously a proponent of atheism, Lewis argued vehemently for his position with colleagues, defending his beliefs. When he read Chesterton's *Everlasting Man*, who was both a Christian believer and one of Lewis' favorite authors,[5] all bets were off. God began to bring people across Lewis' path who he could not ignore. The process had begun. The first phase of this conversion occurred when he could no longer ignore the presence of God that was wooing him. He finally surrendered, but at first, it was simply an acceptance of theism. After that, Lewis continued to resist, but over the course of time, he believed and later wrote, "[I] know *when* it happened but not exactly *how*." He was on a motorcycle heading for the zoo. He said,

> When we set out I did not believe that Jesus Christ is the Son of God, and when we reached the Zoo I did. Yet I had not exactly spent the journey in thought. Nor in great emotion...[6]

TESTING OUR WORLDVIEW

Our worldview can be tested by using the Three Truth Test as presented by R. Totten. There are three qualities that test for the truthfulness of a worldview. First, the worldview must be non-contradictory. Second, if the worldview is inconsistent with human experience and empirical facts of history, nature, or the universe, it fails the truth test. And third, a worldview held by a person must be subjectively satisfactory to that person and livable on a daily basis. If a person cannot or does not live it daily, his inner conviction of the truth is not consistent with his worldview.[7]

In forming a worldview, one must be willing to look within and explore their thoughts and beliefs. They must approach new data with the lens of openness and subjectively weigh its validity according to their personal truth. As we subjectively analyze the data that enters our arena of thought, we must approach it with a willingness to consider how it fits with our worldview but with the respect and courtesy due our "neighbor."[8]

In situations as valuable as face-to-face communication, we must approach the opportunity as a divine appointment to shine our light and be the face of Jesus where it has not been revealed before. Schultze said,

> Speaking and listening to each other is the most intimate and personal way that we commune with each other. Orality opens us up to each other and builds trust.[9]

Lastly, we must remain accountable to our own truth. We have to use the truth test to sift through each idea and hold it captive not only to the Word of God but be willing to examine our own worldview and consider whether it holds up to what we consider to be our Biblical worldview. Examination and analysis of our worldview "can bring about spiritual transformation in the lives of believers."[10]

A significant part of worldview and leadership is knowledge of and willingness to yield to "who" is in charge. In a Biblical worldview, that "who" is God while, in a secular worldview, it is one's self.[11]

SPIRITUALITY

Now more than ever before, there is an increasing interest in spirituality in the workplace. We spend much of our day away from home and at our jobs. People are no longer happy to just collect a paycheck. They want work that is meaningful and significant. The search for meaning has its roots in the advent of technology, downsizing, and organizational restructuring.[12]

> [H]uman resource professionals report dealing with increasing numbers of employees with problems that seem to cross the lines between the spiritual, personal, and professional... Corporate chaplains who number in the thousands represent a booming industry, and careers related to spirituality and counseling in the workplace continue to gain in importance.[13]

Individual's beliefs, values, and moral standards are often based on their religious affiliations or spiritual foundations.

> For many people of religious faith, values are intrinsically woven into their religious faith and training... [and] separating their faith from their moral values might well be impossible.[14]

Extant literature has shown that organizations can benefit from facilitating spirituality in the workplace.[15] The concept of workplace spirituality reflects employee expressions and experiences of spiritiuality at work that are facilitated by various organzational aspects such as culture,[16] organizational climate,[17] leadership,[18] and organizational practices.[19] Scholars posit that spirituality in the workplace not only gives a sense of meaning to their work but encourages a connectedness to others, a sense of community that transcends self, and "inspir[es] a commitment to contributing to others beyond the self in time and place."[20]

A Biblical and spiritual worldview in the workplace enhances employee behavior. Spirituality in the organization encourages connections among employees, "giving them a sense of community, completeness, and joy."[21] Organizations that encourage spirituality will benefit from a more ethical consciousness among employees. Therefore, spirituality in the workplace impacts the organization's culture, climate, leadership, and organizational practices. Workplace spirituality "has a potentially strong relevance to the well-being of individuals, organizations, and societies"[22] and gives to followers a view beyond themselves that builds community, relationships, positive performance, and job satisfaction.[23]

Leaders who have the welfare of their employees in the forefront of their work practices can bring about positive change in the organization by implementing a strategically planned Spirituality Action Plan:

Spirituality Action Plan	
Leader Behavior	**Impact**
Do not define workplace spirituality in religious terms (Harlan, Spirituality in domains and functions of business)	Acceptance by diverse worldviews
Focus on caring for others (Harlan, Spirituality in domains and functions of business)	Transcend self (B. Pawar)
Use a common language (Harlan, Spirituality in domains and functions	Commutes diverse worldviews and

of business)	spiritual beliefs
View individuals as whole persons (Harlan, Spirituality in domains and functions of business)	Creates investment, respect, and caring climate
Create intimate environments (Harlan, Spirituality in domains and functions of business)	Encourages friendly relationships and connectedness
Encourage use of spiritual traits (Harlan, Spirituality in domains and functions of business)	Increases productivity
Memorialize organizational stories (Harlan, Spirituality in domains and functions of business)	Connects to organizational history
Celebrate creativity and give feedback (Harlan, Spirituality in domains and functions of business)	Increases positive relationships
Exhibit ethical standards, lead by example, use integrity, honesty, love, kindness, and respect (Harlan, Spirituality in domains and functions of business)	Models desired follower behaviors & Creates a desirable culture and climate
Show commitment to organization, facilitate employee growth (Harlan, Spirituality in domains and functions of business)	Builds relationships

---

[1] Veith, G. E., 2002.
[2] Ibid.
[3] Ibid.
[4] Ibid., p. 39.
[5] Nicholi, 2013, p. 83.

[6] Ibid., p. 92.

[7] Totten, R., 2004.

[8] Grauf-Brounds et. al, 2008.

[9] Schultze, Q.J., 2000, p. 70.

[10] Naugle, 2002, p. 384.

[11] Gunn, D., 1991, p. 231.

[12] Cash & Gray, 2002, p. 125.

[13] Robertson, G., 1998.

[14] Cash & Gray, 2002.

[15] Pawar, B.S, 2009.

[16] Jurkiewicz &Giacalone, 2004.

[17] Duchon & Ashmos, 2005.

[18] Fry, L.W., 2003.

[19] Pfeffer, 2003, as cited by Pawar, 2009.

[20] Pawar, B.S, 2009.

[21] Ibid.

[22] Sheep, 2006, p. 357.

[23] Van Der Walt & De Klerk, 2014.

8

A LONG ROAD

"More of Him; less of me. More of Him; less of me. More of Him; less of me." This was my mantra as I packed and sorted, wondering what I should take and what I should leave behind. My two small children running around were testaments to my quest to give them a better life.

I had a great job but a low quality of life. The leadership at work was oppressive, and although the job was my livelihood, it felt unbearable to me. I knew too much about the micro-politics of my department, and they weighed heavily on my spirit. There had to be something better than this.

Although I lived in a nice-enough, middle-class neighborhood in America, I read of gang activity in the surrounding community as it had crept in from urban areas to the west. I could not take my children to the park, sit under a tree, and read a book while the children played for fear of losing sight of their blonde heads. Every day, I memorized their clothing and put a big, bright-colored bow in my daughter's hair so she could be easily identified in a crowd.

Child abduction became a very real fear for me when I heard one had happened at a popular, big-name amusement park nearby in which a young child had been snatched from a ride. The abductor had colored the child's hair in the restroom and changed his clothes. An "Amber Alert" had gone into effect quickly, and all entrances and exits were closed to buy time and suppress the abductor's plan. In the end, the child was drugged and carried to an exit over the abductor's shoulder but was recognized at the turnstile by the writing on the bottom of the boy's shoes. Tragedy was averted that day because a parent had wisely chosen his clothing and paid attention to detail.

How does this impact my life? I knew there was something better somewhere with a slower pace and the hope of a less-frantic lifestyle. I wanted that for my children; I needed that for myself.

Spiritually, my life was chaos as well. Although I knew Jesus as my Savior, I struggled with making Him Lord of my life. I came to Him so sorry for my choices while, once again, asking Him to put out the current fire smoldering in my life. Maybe I was running. Maybe I was just getting a fresh start. Maybe a little of both.

Whichever description best fit the situation, I had vowed that I would begin where I landed with a commitment to tithe of my first fruits, something I had struggled with previously. I had begun to study Malachi 3:10, which says,

> "Bring the whole tithe into the storehouse, so that there may be food in My house, and test Me now in this," says the LORD of hosts, "if I will not open for you the windows of heaven and pour out for you a blessing until it overflows."

I had tremendous guilt and sadness. I felt convicted for lack of obedience in the area of tithing. It seemed that, everywhere I turned, someone was asking if I tithed. I knew God was trying to get my attention. And, if I'm honest, I have to say that the second part of that verse intrigued me:

> I will open for you the windows of heaven and pour out for you a blessing until it overflows.

The truth was that, although God did not need my money or my time to make His Kingdom come, I needed His blessing! So, call it bargaining or call it works, I chose to call it "test Me now in this."

Dying Daily

I would like to tell you at this point in the story that what followed my interstate move were blue skies and rainbows. In a literal sense, it was a fitting description, and I am grateful for that aspect of the Pacific Northwest even today, 20 years later. However, the spiritual process I had committed to was more akin to dying.

Arriving exhausted from the journey and certain only of a place to stay at my parents' house, I began. I had no friends and no direction. Unexpectedly, grief washed over me daily. I missed my best friend and confidant, Kathy. I missed the familiarity of the place in which I had spent the last 35 years even though it had become an oppressive and lonely place for me.

We arrived in March, and within just weeks, I received the news that my cousin's life had taken a turn for the worse. Time was short. We had prayed for Diane for years as she battled drug addiction and the resulting Hepatitis C that she contracted. The disease had ravaged her body for many years, and she was now succumbing to its ugliness. Diane had recently given her heart to the Lord, and because of that, we all rejoiced and had peace that we would see her again in eternity. However, there was grief for the years lost and the pain this horrific condition had inflicted on her and everyone who loved her. Losing her at such a young age felt as though we were being cheated. Diane was only 41 years old.

In her last three months of life, healing came in unexpected ways. Hearts were healed, grudges were left behind, and extensions of love surrounded every meeting with Diane. I had not had a relationship with her for many years even though Diane and I had been born within 10 days of each other and had been very close as children. Addiction had changed all of that. However, in her last days, we had renewed fellowship, and I was given opportunities to love her through the mundane tasks that she was unable to do for herself. Symbolic of foot washing, I shaved her legs for her and caught up on some of the laughs we had missed. Diane slipped into Jesus' loving arms just six months after I arrived. It was a Tuesday. We rejoiced that Diane was no longer suffering, but the grief was immeasurable.

Three days after we buried Diane, my cousin Bill (Diane's brother-in-law) died suddenly of a heart attack at the age of 44. Out of love for me, Bill had driven the moving van that was full of all my belongings from my previous home. He was that kind of guy.

I can barely sit still as I write this. Dusting off those memories still hurts. Words flee as I try to express the grief that followed. It came in great tidal waves, washing relentlessly over me with no chance to catch my breath.

FIRSTS AND DAILYS

Needless to say, the entire time since relocating and starting my journey with God afresh, my day-to-day existence had been mired in grief and the "everydayness" of starting life in a new place. Everything was a first: the first time I needed a babysitter, the first time I visited a new church, and even the newness of choosing a new bank, grocery store, and gas station. The firsts seemed endless in the "dailyness" of my life.

It is amazing how much we take for granted in the "dailys." We just move through our day and don't have to think about the established locations we take for granted.

On this journey to establish a better life for the children and me, I had to tackle the minutia of the specifics. In those first months, I found myself traveling to the nearby town almost daily—15 miles west of my little town—because it felt so much bigger. Where I had set up "housekeeping" seemed so sleepy and uneventful that I was drawn to the "big city" nearby. Ironically, the point of this relocation was to live in an environment with less chaos and oppression. The sleepiness was the draw, yet I struggled to live within that environment.

ETCHING AND POLISHING

Jobs eluded me as did direction. I fought it out with God in my bedroom by shaking my fist toward the ceiling. No, I'm not proud of that aspect of our communication, but that is where I was, and He graciously took my anger, heartache, insecurity, uncertainty, grief, and all else that I relinquished. He picked up the pieces and comforted me as I died daily and became more fully alive in Him. I became clay in the Potter's hands. The Potter's wheel was not always kind to me as the Potter reshaped me, but we made progress—slow, slow progress.

Over the course of the past 20 years, He has lovingly changed me. As I let go of bits and pieces of self, He has filled the voids left behind with more of Himself. I wish I could tell you it has been a road traveled with consistent obedience and growth, but it has not. I have proved to myself and to God that I am indeed a slow learner. God has taken me on many journeys through the desert, and I've had more sand in my shoes than I'd like to admit. Shaking the sand from my shoes each time reminds me of who He is and what He's done for me. Each grain of sand paves the way toward a closer relationship with my Lord. Everytime I find myself picking the grains of sand from my hair, I am reminded of the piles behind me that God has led me through. He is beside me in every storm and inhabits the spaces of the atmosphere in which I move. He fills me up and brings wholeness to me as I submit. He gives love to me that I can extend to my neighbor, kindness that I wouldn't have to give without Him.

Again, I say, "More of Him, less of me!"

Back to Malachi 3:10 for a moment as I pull into a rest stop… What a journey it has been, and it clearly has not always been easy. I'm pretty wimpy in the face of challenge and change. I do my share of whining and more than my share of "testing" God. What I have found is that, as I test God in the area of my finances, He has been faithful. I cannot afford to step out from under the fountain of blessing He pours out on me. As a side note, some Biblical translations say He will "pour" out blessing. I prefer the translation that depicts the fountain as a "flood" of blessing. For me, the road to obedience has been littered with pieces of my "self-ness" as I've become more willing to trust Him with financial matters. Although it has been a "sandy" road, it has been even more a refreshing spring of living water that He has flooded over me. Best of all, I have discovered giving as a form of worship to my King. He just loves that!

In His Will

With the children in school and no job as of yet, I sought a ladies' Bible study to understand why I was in this lonely place that I had thought would be so different. I began to attend the study regularly and form some friendships and relationships in the process. Strangely, these ladies were all many, many years my senior. We embarked on an adventure called *Lord I Want to Know You* that was written by Kay Arthur.[1] I was struggling to understand God's will for my life. I had become fearful that, if I made the wrong move, my world would come tumbling down. I needed to know what He wanted for me. Really, I was seeking a sort of insurance policy against more grief.

As we moved through the Bible study, I began to soak up the accumulated wisdom in that room. Relationships formed slowly. I began to understand Esther and Monica as they shared their lives with me. Rhoda was the quirky one, never without one hat or another. Loretta, never soft-spoken, always made me laugh. Cherilyn, also a newcomer, shared about her relationship struggles with her family as well as her health issues. Mostly, what these women and I had in common was a yearning to know more about the Master. And so, I continued to meet with them and share my life. Trust grew in little spurts, and I grew more comfortable in that room.

On a particularly overwhelming and frustrating day, I blurted out, "How can I *know* God's will for my life? How can I be sure?"

After a moment of silence, one person after another began to share with me things that would change my life and the way in which I knew and trusted my God. I will return to this in a little while, but for now, I want to set a Biblical foundation for knowing what God's will is for His children.

What Is God's Will?

As believers in Christ, God has given to us rules to live by, the "Big Ten." With His finger, God chisled out of stone these commandments for the children of Israel:

> You shall have no other gods before Me.
> Do not make idols that look like anything in the sky or on earth or in the ocean under the earth. Don't bow down and worship idols.

Do not misuse My name.

Remember that the Sabbath Day belongs to Me.

Respect your father and your mother.

Do not murder.

Do not commit adultery.

Do not steal.

Do not tell lies about others.

Do not want anything that belongs to someone else. Don't want anyone's house, wife or husband, slaves, oxen, donkeys or anything else. (Exod. 20:2-17, CEV)

Can God's will for His followers be more specific than that? Yes, it can. God has given to us illustrations throughout His Word of what it looks like to be in His will, practical applications for our everyday lives. Jesus instructed His disciples to go into all the world and preach the gospel, a mandate otherwise known as the "Great Commission" (Matt. 28:18-20). Matthew 7:12 tells us, "In everything, therefore, treat people the same way you want them to treat you, for this is the Law and the Prophets," which we commonly refer to as the Golden Rule. In Matthew 22:35-39, being questioned by the Sadducees and Pharisees,

One of them, a lawyer, asked Him a question, testing Him, "Teacher, which is the greatest commandment in the Law?" And He said to him, "'You shall love the Lord your God with all your heart, and with all your soul, and with all your mind.' This is the great and foremost commandment. The second is like it, 'You shall love your neighbor as yourself.'"

Let's recap a little. God specifically tells us to…

- Reach out to others and share the message of Christ,
- Treat others well,
- Love God with everything we have, and
- Love our neighbor

If we are married, God's will for us is to love our spouse in all the ways we are instructed. As parents, we are called to protect and teach our children and to prepare them to "launch" into the adult world of responsibility and independent living. As employees, we are to honor the commitment to do our best in our duties at work and to obey our authorities. We could go on and on.

Returning to my group of ladies now, I can say that what they told me was profound. They assured me that, when we are living in a way that honors God, seeking Him and loving Him, we can be assured that we are in His will. To my cry, "But what if I misunderstand and end up in a ditch (metaphorically speaking)?," Esther assured me with boldness that God would make good out of my bad, citing Romans 8:28:

And we know that God causes all things to work together for good to those who love God, to those who are called according to His purpose.

Suddenly, a "knowing" came over me, melting my heart of fear. The God I was pursuing loved me enough to teach me through my mistakes, pick me up out of the ditch, dust me off, bind my wounds, and set me on my feet again. Oh, what a God we serve. Kind of warm and fuzzy... isn't it? Reminds me of... you guessed it... relationship.

DESIRES OF OUR HEART

When we consider from a more individual perspective what God's will is for our lives—for example, whether or not we should take a particular job, study a specific major, marry or remain single, marry a particular person, etc.— knowing God's will takes on an entirely different perspective.

I know God loves me and wants His best for me. I know His tender mercies, His grace, His forgiveness, and so much more are lavished on me daily, whether or not I am fully aware, in every circumstance in which I find myself. Psalm 37:4 says, "Delight yourself in the Lord; and He will give you the desires of your heart." David, in Psalm 16:11, writes of his Deliverer,

> You will make known to me the path of life;
> In Your presence is fullness of joy; In Your
> right hand there are pleasures forever.

I don't know about you, but I am convinced God will make His will known. Could it be that God's authorship in our lives also plants the seeds of desire when we seek Him and make Him our Lord and Savior? He truly has a plan for each of us (Jer. 31:11).

HE SPEAKS TO ME

Knowing God's "voice" is another matter entirely. Scripture tells us that "His sheep hear His voice and follow Him" (John 10:27). I would say from my own experience that this is not a quick process. I believe that, as we grow in relationship with Him, we become more and more familiar with the voice of God. For the most part, I "hear" God through a "quickening" in my spirit or a "knowing" that takes root in my being and empowers me with confidence I did not know before. Most often, peace follows the knowing or prompting of the Holy Spirit.

I will add a caveat here. When I am prompted by the Spirit of God and recognize the "knowing" I've described, although I have peace, it does not always follow that all fear vanishes. Sometimes, God is stretching me by what He is asking of me, and I am fearful and even dread doing what He's asked me to do. It is then that I have to trust God by faith and move forward. Stepping out in faith and putting aside the fear is not always an easy thing to do.

Serving God requires a refining process that molds us into useable vessels for His purposes. The process is usually difficult and uncomfortable, if not painful. Sometimes, it requires grief and sadness. On the Potter's wheel, God knocks off ugly pieces and smooths out the rough edges. Each time He takes me into the desert, I emerge a little bit smoother as the grains of sand get into nooks and crannies of my life. As I shake the sand out of my shoes after each trip, my life begins to shine brighter in the light of Jesus. Our relationship grows deeper as we take it to the next level.

---

[1] Arthur, K., 2009.

9

WALKING IT OUT

Here's a helpful exercise. On your computer, begin by going to Google.com/earth/ and downloading GoogleEarth®™. This download will take approximately one minute plus another three minutes or so to install the program. Once that is done, you will be looking at a blue image of the world. Now, we have arrived at the facinating part. Type your address in the upper-left-hand corner of the screen, and watch as the application zeros in on your home, the place where you "live, move, and have your being."

As the GoogleEarth®™ program zoomed in on your address from an aerial view, did you notice how tiny your circle of influence is? Of course, many of you have lives that take you all over the globe for work, travel, ministry, recreation, etc. But if we look at this from a purely individual perspective, it paints a clear picture of how tiny we are in the grand scheme of things. This is amazing to me. Most people live their daily lives in a very small world. If you were to draw a circle around my house on GoogleEarth®™, the circumference of that circle would not be very impressive at all. Now, if you zoomed out, my apparent significance would appear even smaller, merely a tiny pinpoint on the earth.

So what is my point? God created the first man, Adam, and gave him the circle of influence that was the Garden of Eden. He and Eve were also but tiny pinpoints on the vast expanse of the earth. And although they were tiny in light of that vastness, God put them there to be in relationship with each other and with Him, to commune with Him and give Him pleasure (Psa. 149:4). He created them from the dirt and said they were "very good." He gave purpose to them, admonishing them to take care of the Garden and everything in it. They were the apple of His eye (Zech. 2:8). Their purpose was to procreate, take dominion over the garden and everything in it, and most importantly to thrive in His presence.

God's Word tells us that God does not change (Mal. 3:6). With that being said, we are also the apple of His eye. He loves us as much as he loved Adam and Eve. He also has a purpose for each and every one of His children. He knew us in our mother's womb and made a plan for each of us (see Psa. 139:13 and Jer. 1:5). And His plan and purpose is not diminished by the size of our dot on GoogleEarth®™.

"God is love" (1 John 4:8). He wants each of us to know Him and to commune with Him. He desires relationship with us, and He pursues us to that end. In the "circle" of relationship that I presented in Chapter Five, when I asked the question, "Who is in the circle?," the answer is a resounding, "God is." He never steps out of the circle. He never gives up on relationship with each of us. Even when we are not entirely present in the circle, God remains. He is immovable in that regard. He stands vigilantly over His purpose for us.

On the GoogleEarth®™ application, imagine if, within each of our circles of influence, we could see God standing as a sentry over each person's circle… and that, as we grow in love for Jesus, our circle moves outward, covering a larger area. Likewise, I am convinced that, as our love for God grows and He sends us further out in an ever-widening circle, we bump into more and more people. We touch lives that we influence, whether we become aware of that influence immediately or never. It is like a "love ripple." Just as a ripple on the water spreads outward from its epicenter, so does His love. What a plan! He can send us near or far, to the grocery store or to the foreign mission field, and our "love circle" follows us and overlaps with others, sometimes becoming the only "love circle" that has ever entered that area at all. To me, this is mind blowing. How great Thou art!

TOUCHING LIVES

What God pours into our lives is what we are to give to others daily. God refines us throughout our lives to become evermore like Jesus. To be more like Him is our highest calling. Living our lives with that purpose in mind creates opportunities for God's love to rub off on the others we touch. I like to think of the "bumping" around that we do as similar to that of a pinball machine. When the little silver ball is launched out of the shoot with the pull of the handle, it careens toward the first obstacle. Upon impact, the ball changes direction and bumps into another obstacle, and on it goes. Likewise, as we "bump around," we influence others.

As lovers of Jesus, we need to shine His light wherever we go. We need to be the person of Jesus that others see. This, of course, largely pertains to those we bump against with some regularity, but it can also be random. I will discuss this a little later.

SHINING THE LIGHT

The semester was at its end, and my student cohort was gearing up for finals. My study group had worked hard to prepare, but none of us felt prepared enough. We had looked at our grades, and one of us—who we will call "Henry"—had methodically determined what each of us would need to score on each final to pass the class in its entirety and what percentage of correct answers we would need to earn the coveted "A." I didn't put much stock in the figures Henry presented because I had prepared and studied my brains out. Regardless of what would happen, I had done all I could do.

Collette and I had known each other for many years, but throughout our bachelor's studies, we had become close. We were both believers and frequently discussed spiritual matters. We prayed for each other and were "study buddies extraordinaire." Henry was solidly in our study group but made no bones about the fact that he did not believe in any of that "God stuff." We continued to pray for him.

On the evening of our first final, as a trio, we entered the classroom and began the test. It was extensive as finals tend to be, and occassionally, one of us would catch the other's eye. The eye contact we made sent the message that none of us could believe this test.

We waited for each other to emerge from the classroom. Of course, I always brought up the rear, being a slow poke when taking tests.

"What was that?" we all asked in unison.

We had each been given a pretest from the professor a week prior to the finals as a tool with which to study.

When we walked into the classroom and were given the final, we heard the words, "You can use your notes."

At first, one or two people looked up with confusion written on their faces.

Being bold, I said, "Would you repeat that, please?"

The professor paused and then repeated those precious words, "You can use your notes to take your final."

A collective rustling of papers took over the atmosphere in the room as everyone opened backpacks and bookbags to retrieve their notes and pretests.

As we opened the test, what we found was even more astonishing and unbelieveable. Every question was identical to the questions on the pretest but with different figures to work from. We stood in the hall, shaking our heads with relief at what had just occurred. Those of us who had used the pretest to prepare had been given the final on a silver platter.

Again, Henry asked, "What was that?"

In unison, Collette and I proclaimed, "That was God, Henry. There is no other explanation. That was God. What do you think now, Henry? Do you believe there's a God now?"

"I will believe it if it happens again for our next final," he replied.

Collette and I nodded in agreement, with smiles on our faces.

The next night, it was the same scenario. We walked into our finance class with fear and trepidation. None of us were confident, and all of us felt unprepared.

Our instructor passed out the finals to each of us and said, "If you have any questions, feel free to ask me."

"Do you mean we can ask you questions about the material on the test?"

"Yes," he replied.

And so began the most amazing final I have ever taken. The evening began as a discussion, not unlike the previous lectures during which we all engaged in conversation about each question. We took turns presenting to the entire class what we each thought of different questions and then were given opportunity to argue for or against the chosen answer to each question. In the hallway that night, Henry was still not convinced, but Collette and I knew without a doubt that we had seen the hand of God at work.

Other bumps with people we encounter are more random. Some of them are significant in the other's life—for example... the kindness you show by allowing someone to go ahead of you in the grocery line or by allowing another driver to enter your lane as theirs is ending ahead. We've all been in these situations. And there are things like stooping to pick up a piece of trash in the parking lot or returning a cart to the cart caddy instead of leaving it beside your car. These are kindnesses that save work for someone else, even when it is that person's job.

We bless others through these kindnesses without knowing the outcome… if there even is one. We touch lives everywhere we go. As God moves among us, present in the very air we breathe, we can extend His love in even these tiny and seemingly insignificant ways. As we move through our dailys, we must be persistent, even at this micro level, in loving our neighbors.

BOLDNESS IN WELL-DOING

Although Henry never did accept Jesus as his Savior, he certainly heard about Him. Collette and I maintained our boldness in well-doing. Throughout our tenure in the cohort program, I made cookies for the class and made extra just for Henry. Collette was the resident well-doer by bringing and sharing, of all things, vegetables, to balance out the desserts I shared. Henry was our concern, and we loved him well. We persisted with boldness as we shared the nature and love of Christ.

BITS AND PIECES AND DIVINE APPOINTMENTS

While I was attending the ladies' Bible study when this journey began, I was living on unemployment and, although my living expenses were low, I struggled to make ends meet. At one of our meetings, when my wallet was empty as well as my fuel tank, I blurted out that I didn't think I would be able to make it to the Bible study the following week because I didn't have enough money to fill my tank with gas, and I had to consider my need to drive my daughter to and from kindergarten for the next five days. It was then that Rhoda—remember that she wore a different hat each week—put on her "blessing hat" and offered her gas credit card to me. My mouth fell open, and tears ran down my cheeks. That was a "bump" that changed me. That was an extension of Christ's love that gave me hope when my situation felt hopeless. And that bump reminds me daily that the small things we do in our daily lives can have profound impact on others. I seriously doubt that Rhoda remembers the events of that day. In fact, I see her around town occasionally, and she doesn't even remember me. But, I remember her.

The lovingkindness that Rhoda shared with me that day was not random. It was a divine appointment. We never know when a bump in the swirl of activity that is our daily lives is random or divine. And for this, we have to make every bump count.

10

DAILY BUMPS

As much as we sometimes might prefer, we cannot move through our lives without relationships. As we discussed before, relationships come in all shapes and sizes. From depth to breadth, they are all different. We must embrace relationships and make them work for us. Let's make them the best they can be, and in so doing, honor our Creator God.

By now, you've likely figured out that relationships can be life-long or brief encounters, or something in between. Relationships can make huge impacts on our lives and are, therefore, solidly imbedded in our memories. They can also be very insignificant—at least, to us. Many never make it into the "saved" file of our memory banks. What is memorable to me may not be memorable to you… and vice versa. Because of this, we must be conscious of every bump in which we are a part.

We are all engaged in a myriad of relationships at any given time in our lives. People come in and out of our lives at warp speed. If we could follow our "bumping patterns" visually throughout our day for a one-week period, we would end up with a tapestry of swirls and curliques that the most creative quilter could not have invented. Of course, the Great Weaver of the universe, the Master of all tapestries, is responsible for that. All of the relationships on each of our individual tapestries would have colors and textures woven in and out that the human eye could not follow. His creativity is not reproduceable. He is unique, just as He has made each of us different from each other. It is unfathomable. I have no doubt that, occasionally, in a restful few minutes, God sits back and admires His handiwork and is blessed by what He sees.

Every day, we are observed by others. Possibly when we least expect it, someone will be watching when we pick up a random piece of trash or offer an umbrella to a young girl pushing a baby stroller in an unexpected rainshower. Someone might also be watching when we throw down that trash or wad of gum or sneak into a parking place that another driver clearly had been waiting for. I write these things not for a guilt trip but to remind us of what matters in our *dailys*.

MERGING

It was mid-day in Southern California. My girlfried Suzanne, her baby Jesse, and I had been out to Fullerton College that morning so I could take care of my next semester's registration requirements. We had walked around the campus on that cloudless, sunny, Orange County day with a toddler in tow.

Preparing for the return trip home, Suzanne and I buckled up. This was in the days prior to the child-seat laws we have today. Because of the absense of a car seat, Suzanne held Jesse in her lap. Returning home, we had not yet hit heavy traffic, but it was beginning to look like gridlock was forthcoming. I was driving my little custom-painted Pearl Blue, 1967 Volkswagon "Bug" at 60 miles per hour in the slow lane. Considering the flow of traffic on the 91 Freeway, that was not excessive. Shortly after entering the flow of traffic on Route 91, I had not yet merged left into the fast lane. Vaguely aware of the position of the cars around me, we cruised along with traffic, singing to the music of The Beach Boys.

As we approached the Harbor Boulevard on-ramp, things changed in a split second as a small red vehicle entered my view. The beat-up little Pinto merged into the lane ahead of me. He entered my lane at the speed of approximately 45 miles per hour. Suddenly, his rear bumper was getting bigger at an alarming rate of speed. Without any forethought, I firmly grasped the wheel and pulled hard to the left to change lanes which, thankfully, was not occupied.

After the Mario-Andretti-like manuever, my car took on a life of it's own. In the blink of an eye, we turned 45 degrees with the nose moving quickly toward the center divider. As we slid sideways in the inside lane, I saw the chain-link divider rapidly approaching. Time had ceased to move normally, and we were now in slow motion. Despite all of my past driving experience, I did what I had never done before... I took both hands off the steering wheel.

I know. I know you're thinking, "How stupid! Don't do it! Hang on, and turn into the skid!"

All I can say is, "It was too late."

The next moment in time was something I will never forget, and I seriously doubt Suzanne has forgotten it either, 40 years later. In the moment when I took my hands off the wheel, a hand as big as a catcher's glove reached down through the roof of my car, grabbed onto my steering wheel, and gave a quick jerk to the right. The cuff of His robe was visible as I watched this magnificent display of strength. Immediately, we stopped skidding, and the car was suddenly going straight in the lane ahead of me. The driver of the red Pinto was most likely oblivious to the drama.

With eyes as big as saucers and our mouths hanging open, I said, "Did you see that, Suzanne?"

She replied, "See what… that we almost died? Well, yeah!"

"No! Not that… the hand."

"I saw your hands weren't on the steering wheel. Geez! What were you thinking?"

"That was the hand of God. He reached down and righted the car in the lane. We have seen the hand of God, Suzanne."

Earilier that day, neither of us had any idea that we would have a near-fatal car wreck, nor did we know that the event would be life-changing. If we had that premonition or knowledge, we would have likely stayed home. I am not aware to this day of whether or not Suzanne was impacted long-term by that experience. I only know that I was.

That day on the 91 Freeway gave new meaning to the saying, "Let go, and let God." We don't know what will happen on any given day. Sometimes, it's good. Other times, it's not so good. What I do know is that not much in our lives happens in a vacuum. We are seen by others and are given opportunities to love them in many different ways. If we can just move around through our "dailys" aware of such bumps and try to give a little extra when we are able, God will be well-pleased. We are not called to be perfect. God is changing us daily into the image of His Son, Jesus. How we handle the bumps we encounter, despite our imperfections, gives us opportunities to be Christ in action.

11

Bringing Your "A" Game

Let's explore the concept of *discipleship*. Merriam-Webster's Dictionary defines a *disciple* as...

> One who accepts and assists in spreading the doctrine of another as (a) one of the twelve in the inner circle of Christ's followers according to the Gospel accounts [or] (b) a convinced adherent of a school or individual.

Bible.org states,

> The Greek term (mathetes) refers generally to any "student," "pupil," "apprentice," or "adherent," as opposed to a "teacher." In the ancient world, however, it is most often associated, with people who were devoted followers of a great religious leader or teacher of philosophy. Though the term "disciple" is used in different ways in the [Bible and the] literature of that time period, there are examples of discipleship referring to people committed to following a great

leader, emulating his life and passing on his teachings. In these cases, discipleship meant much more than just the transfer of information. It referred to imitating the teacher's life, inculcating his values, and reproducing his teachings.[1]

For our purposes, we can deduce that *discipleship* means "following a teacher or adhering to his teachings."

DISCIPLESHIP

The early disciples of Christ, we are told in the *Gospel of Mark*, were ordinary men who Jesus summoned to follow Him. In their committment to Jesus, the 12 disciples left everything they were doing to follow him. As followers, "the Twelve" became intimate friends with Jesus. They spent time with Him, sat at his feet around campfires, traveled with him from one speaking engagement to another, engaged in conversations with Him, and trusted their calling to follow Him. Throughout the process of building relationships with Jesus, they learned from Him and came to know Him as the Son of Man and the Son of God. They believed in Jesus' mission so thoroughly that, when Jesus sent them ahead to spread the Good News, they were willing and obeyed. The entire relationship process was the result of fellowship with the Teacher.

As Christians, we are called to seek Him, know Him, love Him, and obey Him. Callings come in all shapes and sizes as we've discussed previously. Not all of us are called to preach or teach. Some are called to the foreign mission field and others into martyrdom. Regardless of where we are called or how we are called, one calling that is universal is the call to be like Him. As Christians, that is the race we are running.

THE LEARNING CURVE

The operative word in all of this discussion is *commitment*. The call of being in relationship with Christ requires time and willingness. The learning curve for some of us, myself included, is steep, and victory is "hard won."

Each step we take on our journey requires faith. Scripture tells us that to each of us has been given a measure of faith (Rom. 12:3). As we seek Him with our whole mind, soul, and strength, our faith grows (2 Pet. 1:3-5). Sometimes, growing in faith is painful and requires another trip through the desert, causing more gritty, irritating sand to get into our shoes. Becoming holy or being totally devoted to God requires that we learn to trust Him, spend time with Him in prayer, and be obedient in our life choices. We are to seek Him and invest in a relationship with Him. It is a lifelong process.

Jesus has always been in the business of saving the lost. As we are faithful, He uses us to shine His light into this lost and dying world. Earl Creps said, "I suggest that we might refer to lost people not as seekers but as the sought."[2] Each of us was sought by God. We did not stumble into His grace. He has sought us and invested into us since before we were born (Jer. 1:5). He knows the number of hairs on our heads and has been catching our tears in a bottle since the moment of our birth (Matt. 10:30; Psa. 56:8). That is devotion. That is commitment. That is love. That is His holiness.

When We Fail Him (and We Will)...

It took many years of study and prayer for me to know my God enough to actually believe how much He loves me. It was not an easy thing to grasp, and I eventually had to accept it by faith. It was only after I made a conscious effort to believe through faith in His Word that I was actually able to integrate that belief into my heart. Today, I truly understand His love for me and how much mercy and grace He pours out on me daily.

As we trust and obey Him, growing in our understanding of Him, He calls us to shine His light on the world or, at least, the portion of the world in which we have influence. For that calling, He has equipped us for the work He has asked us to do. He asks us to step out in boldness and to do it with excellence (Col. 3:23-24). He wants us to bring our "A" game. With a servant's heart, we must approach the calling with a willingness to serve and consider it a privilege.

Proverbs 1:7 tells us,

> The fear of the Lord is the beginning of knowledge; Fools despise wisdom and instruction.

Despite His instruction, we still fail. Our will gets in the way of His will, and we then suffer the consequences of our disobedience. Hopefully, we can learn the lessons He offers and make better choices the next time He gives us the opportunity to obey Him. Of course, my learning process required a lot of sunscreen as protection against the scorching sun of the desert. It is never pleasant but always done in love. Just as our children don't recognize our discipline toward them as something that is done "for their own good," we know the truth of the statement.

Fearing God was, for many years, my nemesis. I felt as though He was the puppet master, and I was the puppet. I thought that, if I made a bad choice even without intending to, He would strike me or someone I loved dead. However, the fear of God is more properly understood as living in respect, awe, and submission to Him. The fear of God is a way of recognizing our love for Him because, as we seek Him, devote our lives to knowing Him, and serve Him in obedience, our love for Him grows in proportion to our relationship with Him. Amen!

Now, don't get me wrong, my friends; there are consequences for our sin. Some are immediate. For example, if in a moment of anger we lash out at someone and strike the person or a wall, the consequences could be a fractured hand and a fractured relationship.

Other perhaps more insidious sins and their consequences could occur through behaviors we model in front of our children. Years later, we can often see the result of our sin through the actions or attitudes of our children.

And then, there are sins whose consequences creep up on us. This reminds me of the Super Bowl game of 2015. The rivals in that particular game were the Seattle Seahawks and the New England Patriots. In that game, the footballs were deflated below the acceptable threshold, giving Tom Brady (quarterback for the Patriots) an advantage. *The New York Times* reported,

There is less direct evidence linking Brady to tampering activities than either McNally or Jastremski (both Patriot employees). We nevertheless believe, based on the totality of the evidence, that it is more probable than not that Brady was a least generally aware of the inappropriate activities of McNally and Jastremski.[3]

The final score was 28-24, Patriots. I must add a caveat here. I am a die-hard Seahawks fan; however, it is clear to me and to many others that the illegal advantage gained by Brady in that game affected the end score. My point is that, although the Patriots won Super Bowl XLIX, are they really champions? Isn't their "win" tainted by what is widely referred to as "Deflategate"? Didn't the illegal activities of the employee(s) responsible taint the Patriot's "victory"? My answers are "no," "yes," and "yes."

The Patriots' victory was fleeting as word spread and investigations began. And this to say nothing of the impact it had on the Seahawks. Although their loss was a bitter pill to swallow, I have no doubt that the Seahawks felt robbed of an authentic game of skill. Though, Russell Wilson, an outstanding quarterback and a man who professes his Christianity publically, did not have a harsh word. He chose the highroad and did not strike out against the Patriots in any way. He brought his "A" game on the field and off. Go Hawks!

HOLINESS

Holiness is "the state of being holy; purity or integrity of moral character; freedom from sin; sanctity." Boa said,

> Faith is not merely an inward affair of the heart, but it is to be expressed outwardly... Personal and social holiness go together; personal holiness should spill over into our dealings with people and the social order, and social holiness should be embedded in and empowered by personal holiness. [4]

Boa made the point here that Christians are called to be "salt and light to the world" (Matt. 5:13-16). As we are faithful, God allows us to be good stewards of what He has given to us. This includes not only our money but also our opportunities, interests, skills, jobs, talents, families, and everything else. God has placed all of these things in our lives to manage as we move through our dailys and touch others.[5] Let us, therefore, run our race with courage and steadfastness, always seeking to do our best and bring our "A" game for the glory of God.

---

[1] Bible.org.

[2] Creps, E., 2006, p. 58.

[3] Branch, J., 2015.

[4] Boa, K., 2001, p. 240.

[5] Ibid.

12

THE HEART OF THE MATTER

As we near the end of our journey together through this book, I would like to circle back around and address a few points that, although I've touched on in prior chapters, need a little more emphasis.

We are all a part of the "whole" (Rom. 12:6). We don't rotate around the sun alone. We are surrounded by others who are all doing their own thing, living their lives as they see fit, and experiencing the world through individual lenses. Each of us has a worldview that we have adopted as a result of our life experiences. Every one of us sees something different, if only slightly different, and each of us acts according to that worldview.

We touch lives every day. Some of those touches or bumps are significant to us while others are only significant to God or to the person we bumped into.

Being in relationships at work is an important position as we spend eight hours, sometimes more, of each day there. We spend time getting there and getting home. During the commute to and from our workplaces, we often think about... you guessed it... *work*. At home, we try to decompress from our day, and we get ready to return to our workplaces the following morning. Try as we might, we cannot always leave it all there. It is a challenge to be present at home after working all day. It is not an easy transition to make.

STRUGGLES

As long as we walk this earth, we will be bumping shoulders with others, some of like faith and worldview and some who have very different perspectives. As we stroll or "zig-zag" through our everyday lives, we need to pay attention to how we are being perceived in the world. We should walk as though Jesus was walking along beside us because He is. In the dailyness of our lives, whether at home or at work, we must strive to understand other worldviews and belief systems if we expect to reach others and be reached by them. Christians who are invested in spreading the gospel must understand the differences of other people if we want to be effective. This is the purpose of having a servant's heart and being a servant leader. From a servant-leadership theory perspective, we must live out the virtues of humility, love, altruism, vision, trust, empowerment, and service to bring the light of Christ to people who spend such a significant amount of their time in the workplace.[1]

Let's turn to the text in John 20:24-29 and look at a bunch of workers who had the same worldview but struggled individually.

> Now Thomas (also known as Didymus), one of the Twelve, was not with the disciples when Jesus came. So the other disciples told him, "We have seen the Lord!" He said to

them, "Unless I see the nail marks in his hands and put my finger where the nails were, and put my hand into his side, I will not believe."

A week later his disciples were in the house again, and Thomas was with them. Though the doors were locked, Jesus came and stood among them and said, "Peace be with you!" Then he said to Thomas, "Put your finger here; see my hands. Reach out your hand and put it into my side. Stop doubting and believe." Thomas said to him "My Lord and my God!" Then Jesus told him, "Because you have seen me, you have believed; blessed are those who have not seen and yet have believed."

Although not a random bump in a crowd of people nor a brief encounter with a stranger or acquaintance, Thomas experienced an intentional bump with the Divine. This encounter contrasted Thomas' humanity with Jesus' deity through a holy bump literally "into" the Divine. This bump was not a mere shoulder bump but one in which Thomas was able to reach "inside" the wound and feel God's desire to heal his unbelief.

Although God blesses us even when we cannot muster the faith to believe, He prefers that we believe even without a show of miracles. He also knows that, for some people and in certain circumstances, we all struggle with our faith.

The Bible tells us that the wound in Jesus' side was made by the sword of a Roman soldier in an attempt to determine whether or not the Son of God was truly dead. In doing so, prophecy was fulfilled (Exod. 12:46; John 19:33). This prophecy foretold that Christ was the sacrificial lamb that would save us from our sins, as the Passover meal represents. However, He also knew that, even those with whom He had spent the past three years still struggled in their humanity. Could it be that God had another motive for the piercing of Jesus' side? Could it be that God knew that, in the moment of Thomas' grief and doubt, being invited by the Teacher to put his hand inside the wound would be what Thomas would need to truly believe? I think so.

Imagine for a moment how the days of Thomas' life unfolded after that "holy bump." Following that encounter with the risen Lord, the God of the universe, Thomas not only believed but was transformed in his belief system and boldly moved forward to make every bump count.

ENCOUNTERS

"Okay, God... You better send me an angel because there is nobody around to help me." This was the prayer I prayed in the concrete parking structure at UCLA Medical Center. My husband of just a few months had recently been diagnosed with bone cancer and was having a round of chemotherapy... again.

Holding down a full-time job all week long and taking care of Sam's little girl was definitely a struggle. Each evening after work, I would drive from the outskirts of suburbia over five freeways and absolute gridlock to be with my husband as the chemo took him to the brink of death. Then, with the use of antidotes against the poison put into his system, the doctors would bring him back to a place in which his body could survive and heal until the next round two weeks later. It had been a grueling struggle. If I wasn't driving, working, or trying to sleep, I was taking mid-night phone calls from Sam's intoxicated aunt as she sobbed into the phone and told me how sorry she was that Sam was sick. Sam's parents were in denial about his condition but often did the "day-shift visitation" while I worked at my job.

During that time, I felt very alone. My family rallied around me. My mom picked up my stepdaughter from school, fed her, and put her to bed while waiting for me to pick her up sometime in the late evening when I would resume my motherly duties. It was a blessing to be sure. But on the other side of the coin, I found an interesting phenomenom taking place. Most of my friends didn't know what to say, so they said nothing. They were unable to step into my grief, hold my hand, and walk in it.

I was still driving my 1967 customized Volkswagon with an aftermarket radio. It was a sunny Saturday as I listened to the music and drove into the UCLA parking structure on my way to visit Sam. I found a parking spot near the entrance that forced me to park on a slight incline. From that parking spot, it took me approximately 15 minutes to walk to Sam's hospital room.

Several hours later, I returned to my car to start the trip back home. By that hour, the parking structure was deserted. Exhausted from the week, the drive, and the emotional visit with Sam, I got in my car, buckled my seatbelt, and turned the key. Nothing! My heart sank. Already emotionally exhausted, I was very short on patience for such a snag as a dead battery.

When I had entered the parking structure, the radio reception was interrupted, and because I hadn't heard it, I had forgotten to turn the radio off. Not completely defeated, I rallied my thoughts. My plan was to 1) put the car in reverse, 2) release the emergency brake, 3) let the car begin to roll backward down the very short incline, and 4) pop the clutch. It was a viable option, but it was unsuccessful because the incline was not steep enough or long enough to get enough speed for a compression start. And so, my solution had failed as I came to a stop in the middle of the parking lot, now on level ground and without options.

I was too angry and frustrated with God even to cry. I had prayed my heart out that God would intervene in this whole cancer mess. I didn't understand why He would allow such a disease to ravage my young husband's body, but He had. Not only had we struggled with the work issues, insurance, medical bills, chemotherapy, radiation therapy, and major surgery to remove the cancerous diseased bone and replace it with a cadaver bone, we had just been told that there was a spot on Sam's lung that the doctors had been watching. They then confirmed a diagnosis of metastatic lung cancer. The cancer had spread, an even more serious and frightening concern than the original diagnosis of osteogenic sarcoma.

That was where my heart was when I found myself stranded in the parking lot. Alone. Always alone. That was when I shouted at God and told Him to send me an angel to get me out of this mess. I just wanted to go home. Without further options, I looked in the rearview mirror to be sure there were no cars behind me. I put the car in neutral and got out. I was going to push the car as best I could to get some momentum, jump in, pop the clutch, and try again to get enough compression generated to start the engine.

I had just begun to push when I glanced around behind me. That was when I saw him, a "man" silently approaching my car. He said nothing, but he communicated without words that I should get in the car. Relieved, I did just that. He began to push, I popped the clutch, and the engine turned over. I put the car in neutral and got out to thank my rescuer, but he was nowhere to be seen. He had vanished without a trace as quickly as he had appeared. I looked everywhere, but there was no place to hide. The structure was huge and open. He had simply disappeared.

DIVINE BUMPS

In that moment, I was changed. I wish I could tell you that Sam had no further complications or surgeries after that divine encounter, but I cannot. What changed for me was knowing that, when I called on God, He heard me. He had answered my call that day in an instant. I no longer doubted that He was present and on His throne. I hunkered down into that knowledge and hung on for what would continue to be a "white-knuckle" experience for some time to come. As the psalmist David cried out, so did I:

> The cords of death encompassed me, and the torrents of ungodliness terrified me. The cords of Sheol surrounded me; the snares of death confronted me. In my distress I called

upon the LORD, and cried to my God for help;
He heard my voice out of His temple, and
my cry for help before Him came into His
ears.
(Psa. 18:5)

God was still on the throne, and for whatever reason He had allowed this cancer to come into our lives, I was strengthened.

My personal struggle during those years was very difficult. I struggled in my life with health issues and with my faith. The conditions and concerns of my life continued to spiral downward, and still He was there. During those turbulent years, I continued to make less-than-great choices, but I did not ever wonder if God was there or if He was able. Thomas was a doubter… just like me. I had come to a point where I measured my importance and the importance of my relationships by the circumstances in which I lived.

The similarities between my life and Thomas' life were parallel journeys, separated by a mere 2,000 years. Thomas and I both met the Master and experienced the touch of His divinity in a special way. I did not touch His nail-scared hands or put my hand into His side as Thomas had. But that day in the parking structure, I certainly felt the touch of the Healer's hand. He picked me up as a bruised, bloody, whimpering, and uncertain mess. And instead of reaching into His wound, He reached into mine. His desire? To heal me and move me toward wholeness. That was and is the heart of the matter.

[1] Patterson, K., 2003.

13

TRUST AND OBEY

G od puts a premium on trust and obedience. In whatever our calling, the Bible tells us over and over again to trust and obey God. One of the most well-known Scripture passages and one that is on my short list of favorites is Proverbs 3:5-6:

> Trust in the LORD with all your heart and do not lean on your own understanding. In all your ways acknowledge Him, and He will make your paths straight.

Countless times, I have found myself in an uncomfortable and even painful situation that I did not understand or could not reconcile. Inevitably, I found myself in this proverb as I tried to navigate the current struggle. Whether a medical condition, relationship issue, or even a work-related issue, I have found that I struggle to walk in trust, as the problem persists. When I cannot understand the circumstances, I have to be reminded that I cannot trust my own understanding.

THE LUMP AND ITS BUDDY

Sitting in the dentist chair with a bib around my neck, I waited for my dentist to examine me at my six-month check up. I have never struggled with "dentist anxiety," so I was very relaxed. This was a routine visit, but I wanted to be sure to mention the little lump on my tongue again as I had at the previous three or four visits. I wasn't alarmed, but as an advocate for "knowing my body," I wanted him to examine my tongue that day as well.

At every prior visit, my dentist had taken a quick peek at it, felt it, and said it was nothing to worry about. So, as I waited for him to come into my cubicle, I kept it in the forefront of my mind so I wouldn't forget to mention it and have him look at it again.

He entered, sat down, and said, "Hi, Barb. How are you? Any concerns today?"

With his instruments in my mouth, I attempted to answer. "Nothing much except the little lump on my tongue."

"Haven't we looked at it before?" he asked as he began to look at it.

I attempted to answer the question, now with his fingers holding my tongue.

"Yes, you've looked at it several times and assured me that it was nothing to worry about. The only thing that concerns me is that the little lump now has a "buddy" right next to it."

With that said, more probing began with earnest. What came next gave me a bit of anxiety.

"I want to send you to an oral surgeon to have another look."

I moved through the rest of that day with a nagging concern in the back of my mind. I wondered why he was never worried about it before, but all of a sudden, he seemed concerned. I called the oral surgeon for an appointment immediately. When I finally got in for my exam, I was feeling fairly calm about the whole thing, having had some time to process it.

"Well, what do you think, Doctor?"

"I think I need to remove these lumps, Mrs. West."

Still feeling slightly upbeat, I said, "Okay. Are you concerned?"

"Yes. I'm always concerned with patients that are referred to me."

Suddenly, I was not upbeat at all. A cold veil of fear descended on me and pushed my heart and mind into a tail spin that would take me on a wild ride.

Over the course of the next couple of weeks, not only was I fearful concerning my health but I encountered unexpected insurance issues. Because the surgery was to be done in the surgeon's office, my medical insurance would not cover it. They were calling it a "dental" procedure. Because the surgery was not routine and outside the normal purview of dentistry, my dental coverage was not helping much at all. The bottom line? Most of the cost was going to come out of my pocket. More anxiety poured over me! At that point, I clearly had no options. I needed the surgery, but it was going to cost more than I could afford… more than I had.

When facing serious health issues, I tend to depend on my mother for strength. However, this time, she was away in Romania. I prayed and sought God during those dark days prior to the surgery and after it as I waited for the biopsy reports. My fear was palpable and overshadowed my days and my nights. I researched what the recovery would be and the ramifications of a bad biopsy report. It wasn't pretty. I grappled with the thought of losing at least a large section of my tongue. Tongue loss would inhibit me from being able to push food to the back of my throat for swallowing, impact my ability to speak, and inhibit my ability to taste. Maybe some would call my research obsessive or bordering on a "doom-and-gloom" attitude. But regardless, I had to *know* and prepare myself for the possibilities. When my surgeon is concerned, I am concerned.

One day, I sat down at my piano, and with my very limited skill level, I began to play "He Is Able" over and over again.

He Is Able
by Greg Ferguson

He is able more than able
To accomplish what concerns me today
He is able more than able
To handle anything that comes my way
He is able more than able
To do much more than I could ever dream
He is able more than able
To make me what He wants me to be

Every chord began to infuse me with hope, reassure me of His ability to take care of me, and give me peace. God commands us to trust Him for all things. Psalm 4:5 says, "Offer the sacrifices of righteousness, and trust in the

LORD." In his *New American Standard Study Bible*, John MacArthur wrote that "trust is a commitment to faith." As I offered the sacrifice of worship to my God and sang the song that proclaimed His ability to take care of *anything* that concerned me, I became obedient to Him to trust Him, love Him, and honor Him. My focus shifted from myself to my God. God began to fan the flames of faith within me as I committed to trust Him.

It would not be fair to end the story there, so I will share with you what happened after the surgery. After the operation, I sported an inch-long incision on the top of my tongue in which I proudly wore six black stitches with 1/2" long "tails" on them. Because the suture material was rigid, they all stood straight up on my tongue. At the time, I was working at an elementary school where I encountered children throughout my day. One day at recess, I asked one of the particularly "feisty" little boys if he wanted to see something really gnarly. Of course, he was all in. So, I stuck out my tongue, and he was duly impressed. For the rest of that week, he brought his friends around at every recess to see my "Franken-tongue."

A week later, my biopsy results came back negative for malignancy. The original lump was a tiny piece of glass, and its "buddy" was a tiny sliver of wood that my body had done its best to wrap in a protective layer of tissue that had formed both lumps. Crazy joy filled my heart that day. Although I was baffled as to how the wood and glass had embedded themselves in my tongue—as I was not in the habit of licking handrails or dragging my tongue along the ground—but I no longer cared. My God was able. I had committed to trust Him by faith, and He had taken care of the issues.

OBEDIENCE

Obeying God is the outward manifestation of loving Him and trusting Him. Often times, if we did not trust in God and believe in His omnipotence, omnipresence, and omniscience, we would have a great deal of trouble obeying Him.

Our obedience says a lot about our relationship with God. Dallas Willard wrote,

> Actions do not emerge from nothing. They faithfully reveal what is in the heart... It is easy to clean the outside of a cup without washing the inside, but it is hard to wash the inside thoroughly and leave the outside dirty. Washing the inside has as its natural accompaniment the cleansing of the outside. Only a spot here or there may be left.[1]

Eugene Petersen translates the passage of Joel 2:12-14 as follows:

> But there's also this, it's not too late—
> GOD's personal Message!—
> "Come back to me and really mean it! Come fasting and weeping, sorry for your sins! Change your life, not just your clothes. Come back to GOD, *your* God. And here's why: God is kind and merciful. He takes a deep breath, puts up with a lot, this most patient God, extravagant in love, always ready to cancel catastrophe. Who knows? Maybe he'll do it

now, maybe he'll turn around and show pity. Maybe, when all's said and done, there'll be blessings full and robust for your GOD! Change your life, not just your clothes."

At the close of an evangelistic outreach in 1887 featuring the preaching of Dwight L. Moody, a young man stood and gave his testimony of salvation during the meeting that night. He had no previous experience with church, religion, or anything like it. At the close of his testimony, he said, "I'm not quite sure. But I'm going to trust and obey." As a result of those words, John H. Sammis penned the words to the well-known hymn that we know today by the same name. Although the entire song expresses the point of trust and obedience, take a closer look at the opening verse and the closing verse.[2]

Trust and Obey
by John H. Sammis

When we walk with the Lord in the light of
    His Word,
What a glory He sheds on our way!
While we do His good will, He abides with
    us still,
And with all who will trust and obey.

Refrain:
Trust and obey, for there's no other way
To be happy in Jesus, but to trust and obey.
Not a shadow can rise, not a cloud in the
    skies,

But His smile quickly drives it away;
Not a doubt or a fear, not a sigh or a tear,
Can abide while we trust and obey.

Not a burden we bear, not a sorrow we share,
But our toil He doth richly repay;
Not a grief or a loss, not a frown or a cross,
But is blessed if we trust and obey.
But we never can prove the delights of His
    love
Until all on the altar we lay;
For the favor He shows, for the joy He
    bestows,
Are for them who will trust and obey.
Then in fellowship sweet we will sit at His
    feet,
Or we'll walk by His side in the way;
What He says we will do, where He sends we
    will go;
Never fear, only trust and obey.

God refines us through circumstances in our lives, washing our insides clean of self and the human characteristics that bind us. The deeper we move into relationship with Him, the more we will want to please Him through serving and loving those around us. We become His hands and His feet. Through the refining process, He blesses us and others. As He cleans our outsides, He makes every bump count.

[1] D. Willard, 1997.
[2] Christianson, C.R., 2016.

14

THE MAGNOLIA PRINCIPLE

PRAYER

According to *Merriam-Webster's Dictionary*, *prayer* is "a solemn request for help or expression of thanks addressed to God or an object of worship."

There are three types of prayer: invocation, intercession, and devotion:

> A prayer of invocation is one in which the pray-er asks an authority figure for something or for assistance. The prayer of intercession asks for something for someone else, and a prayer of devotion expresses love, loyalty or enthusiasm about someone or something from the pray-er to the pray-ee.[1]

> Prayer is conversation with God; the intercourse of the soul with God, not in contemplation or mediation, but in direct address to him.[2]

I think we get the picture. When we pray, we are in communication with our Lord. Because He is, after all, the master of relationship. He listens when we speak to Him. He not only hears the words we say, but He understands the heart of our prayers and what our purpose is when we pray.

Prayer is important to God, so much so that He gave us instructions on how to pray. We refer to His instructions as "The Lord's Prayer," which was taught in the Sermon on the Mount. Although I have attempted to pray the Lord's Prayer many times, I often find that my prayers are scattered all over the place. For years, I've felt poorly about my prayers because they don't often line up directly with Christ's model. However, when we look at prayers that wander in a rather unsystematic way or seemingly without direction, it seems to me that it does mimic conversation with a friend.

FRIENDING

Many times in Scripture, Jesus refers to those who follow Him as His friends (John 15:14-15). Personally, I find this very freeing. I struggle at times with our contemporary concept of what a friend is because most people have few friends and many acquaintances. We often use the term *friend* pretty liberally and oftentimes with little descretion. However, I believe that the true implications of "friending" are a mutual respect for one another and a desire for a friend's good, loyalty, and trust. If we apply these characteristics to God, we will discover that God considers Himself a friend to us.

God being a friend to us required the Son, who was fully God, to leave His heavenly home willingly and become fully human. This is a miraculous feat in and of itself, but there is more. God didn't just pop into mortality beside us one day to become our friend, but He came as a baby. He came as *we* arrive, through the birthing process. He endured diapers, colic, teething, childhood, adolescence, and all the rest. It was because of this sacrifice that He became our friend.

WHY BOTHER?

So why do we pray? Again, I have to liken it to friendship and relationship. God wants to communicate with His children, and He wants His children to communicate with Him, not out of obligation but out of desire to connect with Him.

My grandson is such an important part of my life. I love to spend time with him and talk about him. And blessings on you if I see you in person because I always "just happen to have pictures!" But what blesses me from the top of my head to the tips of my toes is when he tells his mommy that he needs to see MawMaw. When he just can't stand to be away from me another day and has an abundance of "stuff" to tell me, it melts my heart.

Dreyson doesn't have a terrific command of the English language yet. I just say he speaks Swahili or whatever language I can't understand. I have to listen closely to what he says, and often, I have to ask his mommy for translation. But usually, I get the message behind his words. I want to understand what he is saying because I love him, and I want to communicate with him. I want to hear his heart and understand what goes on in that little three-year-old head. When Dreyson was an infant, I spent a lot of time talking to him and playing with him.

But mostly, I made eye contact and just loved on him. We rocked and cuddled. I sang to him and read to him. At that tender age, he didn't understand my words, but he understood my heart.

It is the same with God. He wants to cultivate the same kind of relationship with you, one that oozes with love... one that shares the happy and the sad... one in which we desire His presence enough to run back to Him, frequently. One difference with divine friendship is that He is always available. He never tells us to call back later when He has an opening in His schedule. He never sleeps, and he consistently yearns to communicate with each of us.

Sometimes, it seems as though our prayers are not being answered... as though God is on vacation or something. In those times, we must be steadfast in our efforts to come to Him. We must believe that He hears us and continue to pour out our heart to the One we seek. When we think He isn't listening, we will realize later that He was listening and did answer us. Often, when I look back over the past few weeks, months, or even years, I see His hand at work. In these times of reflection, we are able to see changes that, although possibly subtle at the time, moved circumstances in response to our prayers. At other times, we look back and see that circumstances have changed, and we are glad that, in His infinite wisdom, our request was denied.

Whether answered in the way we had hoped or not, prayer changes our hearts. Fervent, effectual prayer aligns our hearts with God's. When alignment takes place, we have peace, and the attitudes of our hearts allow God to mold us into who He wants us to be and prepare us for His purpose (Jam. 5:16). Our relationship with God becomes more intimate, and we grow. We tuck in a little tighter to His embrace. I often conjure up an image of God and me, not dissimilar to when my grandbaby snuggles into my lap and I envelop him in my embrace. I tuck his little feet under my afgan, gently push his head to my shoulder, and rock us back and forth while singing or humming one of his favorite songs. In this posture, he is comforted. His ear connects with the steady, slow rhythm of my heart. In those times of communion, we become one. Peace, joy, and an intimate satisfaction pour over me. What could be better? God wants communication with each of us to be like that: fulfilling, comforting, and something that we cherish as His child. Try it. You'll like it.

OBEDIENCE AND THE WAITING

God is patient with our imperfections. I tend to think that—as I commune with God, become obedient to His Word, and become equipped for His purposes—the equation should culminate in action. I struggle with the attitude of "I've done my part… now, You do yours." I know that sounds very unspiritual, but let me explain.

When God puts something on my heart, at first, I'm unsure. So, I pray and think and, to my shame, not always in that order. As my prayers continue over time, I become convinced (or not) that I am being led by the Holy Spirit. And as prayer follows on the heels of prayer, my heart begins the alignment process, and a boldness follows. After all, Psalm 32:8 tells me,

I will instruct you and teach you in the way
which you should go; I will counsel you with
My eye upon you.

But the process is often not complete—at least, not
from my perspective. I'm anxious to rip open the package
and see what's inside. I am ready to jump in and get
started. I don't want to wait. I want to "Just Do It" as the
Nike™ slogan says. Sometimes, God has other ideas, and
His ways are frequently not my ways. So, the waiting
begins.

MORE WAITING

I've always been a strong woman—at least, on the outside.
On the inside, I'm soft and pretty whimpy. I tend toward
overthinking and analyzing things to death. Because of
these character traits, I've become adept at "making things
happen" for better or for worse.

It was the week preceding Mother's Day of 2012, and
my husband had been in the hospital for weeks. At that
time in his long ordeal following an infected hip
replacement, this was not unusual. It seemed he was in the
hospital more than he was at home. We hadn't celebrated
an anniversary, Mother's Day, Father's Day, or any other
holiday with the exception of Christmas for the past two
years due to his frequent hospitalizations. We were weary
of it all. During one of my hospital visits, I asked him if he
would get me a tree for Mother's Day that year. He said he
would but that I would have to buy it, plant it, etc.

I had been wanting a Magnolia tree for a long time and
was itching to see those magnificent white flowers

blooming in my yard. With his blessing, I went ahead and made it happen.

Oh, how I lovingly ministered to my tree. I watered and fertilized it with tender-loving care. It did not bloom that summer, and although most people would have guessed it would not bloom the first season after planting, I held out hope. I was becoming impatient. Through the fall, I watched as it did nothing. So, I went to the nursery and asked about its progress, and they were very unimpressed with my concern. So I waited and watched for what seemed like too long.

On a cool and slightly blustery fall morning, after my Bible reading and study, I put on my slippers and robe and went out in the early-morning hours to my Magnolia tree. In the solitude of that moment, I laid my hands on that tree and prayed with all my might, fully believing that my tree would bloom and not die. Through the winter, I watched and prayed.

In the spring of the following year, I went on an outing with my church. These outings were called "Great Adventures" and were offered several times each year as an opportunity for anyone who wanted a break from the everydayness of their lives to jump on a bus and be transported to a museum or a garden. On this particular day, we went to the tulip fields in LaConner, Washington. I had not been there for many years and was looking forward to it. As usual, the ladies chatted and joked while the pastor did the driving. During one of these conversations, I mentioned that my Magnolia had not yet bloomed while others in my neighborhood already had.

It was then that the disheartening words were offered: "Maybe it just takes a few years after being planted to bloom?" These words were the scourge of my whole belief system as it applied to my tree.

So I blurted out, "Oh, no. Don't say that. I laid hands on my tree and prayed that God would make it bloom. I can't wait for several or even a few years to see it bloom."

You can imagine the atmosphere in the bus at that point. Some looked at me as though I was being a bit crazy and were thinking... well, I'm not really sure what they were thinking. Others, like my good friend Samm, just started laughing. She thought I was joking. I was not!

Needless to say, my faith was challenged that day, and I began to doubt the effectiveness of my fervent prayer for my tree. Now, I know it's a bit unusual to pray for a tree, but I am a bit unusual as well. Plus, I felt it was scripturally-sound thinking and action. After all, Jesus prayed for (or, cursed, in this case) a fig tree, and His prayer came to pass (Matt. 21:19-21). So I concluded that praying for my tree was evidence of my faith. Maybe it sounds like I'm trying to justify my "unusualness"—or, as my children would say, "dorkiness"—and maybe I am, but the story does not end there.

Daily, I checked on "Maggie." I vigilantly watched the unfurling of new leaves as they emerged from their pod-like covers. There were many of them. I know because I counted them. I watched the old leaves that were yellowing with age and dropping to the ground, but I was encouraged with the new foliage I saw that was replacing the old with new. Throughout the weeks of spring that slowly turned to summer, my hopes were high that God was answering my prayer.

Then, upon inspection one day, I saw what looked like a different type of pod. I looked closely, and this was a much more conical-shaped pod rather than a twisty type of pod. I watched diligently and saw that it was opening differently than the leaves had. Oh, how I rejoiced. Redemption! Truly, that was how I felt. Finally, the waiting was over, and God had answered my prayers. Although the life of a Magnolia flower is very short, the time it takes to open from pod to bloom is a bit lengthy, especially when you are nearly camping out beside it to watch. I was obsessed. I didn't want to miss a thing.

Eventually, the green pod covering began to peel open and split at a snail's pace. On approximately the ninth or tenth day of this process, I saw my opportunity to help speed the process along. Ever so gently, I peeled back the layer of pod that was taking so long to expose the blossom I had been waiting to see for at least a year. And then, it happened. The only blossom on the entire tree broke off in my hand! Here is where I would expect to hear a collective gasp or sigh. I picked up that broken and immature flower and went inside to pout. I was heartbroken.

In my grief—and, yes, there was grief—scriptures began to roll into my consciousness. I opened my Bible to Psalm 37 and began to read.

> Trust in the LORD and do good; dwell in the land and cultivate faithfulness. Delight yourself in the LORD; and He will give you the desires of your heart. Commit your way to the LORD, trust also in Him, and He will do it... Rest in the LORD and wait patiently for Him... Wait for the LORD and keep His way, and He will exalt you to inherit the land.

I know that some of you are saying that these verses have been taken out of context because the psalmist wasn't praying to God about some Magnolia tree but about the security of those who trust in the Lord versus the insecurity of the wicked. But if you will just indulge me for a moment, maybe I can explain.

You see, using my own "strength," I had rushed the process. I knew that God would have "given me the land" and "given me the desire of my heart" if only I had waited. My impatience was the reason I did not see that blossom come into bloom. There was a significant lesson in this for me.

God was teaching me that I can't fix everything. He threw in quite a bit of "my timing is perfect" and a good dose of "rest in the Lord and wait patiently for Him." I thought of the application of these Biblical truths for my life. I saw how I had rushed into many things in my life that I was sure He was directing me toward. And then, there were those things I had rushed into and made happen that He was not directing me toward. As He reminded me of His sovereignty and majesty in the "things of this life," He nurtured and lovingly cared for my brokeness... not the brokeness of the Magnolia, which was a small illustration of my impatience... but of the wisdom and freedom that comes from waiting on Him. As I waded through the mire I had created at different times in my life, I began to recognize things that I had pushed for prematurely. These were things that would have turned out better if left to Him. They were times when, instead of speaking, I should have been listening.

I was not good at resting in Him. I was good at rushing ahead of Him. Oh, how different things might have been had I rested in Him and listened instead of acted. I had always pushed on partly-closed doors, and occasionally, God had allowed me to push them open, ending in a result that was allowed by God but was not His best for me. Because of His love for me, He had rescued me and pulled me out of the "ditches" of my own making. In each case, He picked me up and brushed me off and set my feet on the ground again. I learned that relationship is a two-way street. It is giving and taking, talking and listening, trusting and obeying, and resting and waiting. I have to listen as much as I talk, and if I don't hear Him, waiting and resting in Him will be my best and least-painful option.

REDEMPTION

I would be remiss if I ended the story here. The following summer in 2014, my husband was recovering from another surgery that was designed to save his leg and close a gaping wound. He was admitted to a nursing home for what turned out to be almost six months in duration. Going to visit my husband in the nursing home was difficult. The atmosphere was sad. People were sick, and many were afflicted with dementia or other diseases that had robbed them of their ability to care for themselves. After a short time in the nursing home, he too became lethargic and hopeless. He slept all day everyday, awakening only for personal needs and meals. During those days, I had to coordinate his care because the nursing home was lacking in that area. His doctor visits were not in our local area, so we were forced to transport him by ambulance each time. It was a very discouraging time for me, for him, and for my son, David.

After about a month in the nursing facility, I began to notice changes in my yard. It was coming to life again and bursting with the colors of spring and summer. As days turned into weeks, I also began to notice changes in "Maggie" as well. Her leaves began to perk up, and new leaves showed themselves. And then, on a sunny summer morning, I noticed a blossom pod and then another. I was thrilled. I watched them, but I did not touch them.

Over the course of the next couple of months—in the bleakest of times during my husband's surgeries, treatments, and numerous setbacks—my Magnolia tree became a riot of blooms. Every day, a new one opened, and I could always count at least 10 or 12 blooms present at any given time. To others, it might seem like a nice thing to see my Magnolia tree in bloom. They might think, "Oh, isn't that lovely. Look how big those flowers are, and the smell is heavenly." But to me, it was much more. It was much much more. It was a moment that I would have to say was a divine appointment with my God.

Seeing the tree in bloom gave me hope when all else seemed hopeless. God ministered to me during that time when it seemed my world was falling apart. He showed me that He cared and that He remembered. He reminded me that His timing was the best timing. He showed me His lovingkindness through a simple flower that lasted only four days when it bloomed, but that was beautiful and joyous in its time. He showed me that, when I delight myself in Him, He is faithful to give me the desires of my heart.

As of this writing, it is July once again. The new green foliage has opened, and there are many bright-green leaves emerging. And yes, there are flower blossoms in the process of opening. There are four I've counted, but I never touch. Everytime I go out to my yard to check on my Magnolia tree, I am reminded of God's goodness and His care for me. I can't say that it is any easier to wait, but I rest more in the waiting now, and I look for the joy redemption brings.

---

[1] Christian Answers.net, 2016.
[2] Ibid.

15

THE RETURN TRIP

Thank you for making this journey with me and staying the course. As a passenger or observer, at least, I have dragged you over "hill and dale" on my journey. I have dragged you through my sand dunes and valleys of shame but always with the gift of God's grace and Jesus at the end of each detour, standing with His arms spread wide to welcome me at the finish line. Through every failure I have experienced, I could hang my head and cower because of the choices I've made. However, in the light of Jesus, I choose to hunker down and embrace the lessons I've learned.

I am no less anxious to run too quickly and to fix what I determine needs to be fixed. I struggle to keep my thoughts to myself and not to blurt out every thought that enters my head. I still war with my mind over thoughts that are not becoming to any person, whether Christian or not, and I still make mistakes that, in retrospect, were "no-brainer" signs that I ignored. I am still very skilled at ignoring the flashing red lights and the subtle red flags strewn strategically along the path of my life. And because of the trappings of the world that stick to me relentlessly, I still find myself slogging through the desert with sand in my shoes, wishing I had remembered the sun screen.

However, as I move through each desert experience, I accept the process more and fight it less. I thirst more for the living water that He provides and go into each trip around Mount Sinai a little better equipped to absorb the lesson and move forward. Each trip seems to find me kicking and screaming less and bowing my knee in the hot sand more frequently and earlier in the journey.

I realize that I am not in another desert experience because I am bad, worthless, or in need of punishment but because of God's love for me. He disciplines those He loves (Heb. 12:6). I understand that He wouldn't bother with me if He didn't love me. Do the sand storms get more enjoyable? No. I still hate every grain of sand I find in my shoes or in my hair. Do I complain less and act differently because of the latest desert excursion? Yes, sometimes. I try to grasp the breadth and depth of His love for me. I try to figure out what the purpose in my current sand journey is so I can shorten the trip if at all possible. I try to figure out how learning the current lesson can change me into the person God intends me to be. I am commited to running the race He has set before me and to glorifying Him at the finish line.

INTERCHANGES

I was 17 years old and on my way to Los Angeles. I had not driven the freeways much; I hadn't needed to. If you have driven there, you know that, if there is no gridlock to contend with at that particular hour, traffic moves quickly and does not allow for rapid course adjustments. Strictly speaking, if you don't know where you are going, you are likely lost. I was on a shopping mission to downtown Los Angeles. I had no companion that day to navigate for me or lend expertise. My father, being very familiar with the Los Angeles freeway system, had told me which freeways to take to find my way. I was confident that, by following his directions, I would get there and back without a hitch. It wasn't long before I found out differently.

I had successfully navigated the interchange from the 91 Freeway West to the 605 Freeway North without incident or a spike in blood pressure. I had traveled these two freeways and was familiar with them. As I was swept along in the swift flow of traffic, I noticed the big green sign ahead that said PASADENA. Here is where it got sketchy for me.

I didn't want to go to Pasadena. I was going to Los Angeles. My father had not told me I would encounter this option. Without freeway skills and navigational savvy, I wasn't aware that, as soon as I would take the I-5 North option, I would have the Pasadena option as well as the Los Angeles option. At that point, I only knew that I *didn't* want to go to Pasadena. Fortuntely, the Los Angeles option came into view shortly after I had veered west onto the I-5. I managed to stay the course and end up where I had intended to go but not without sweat on my brow.

I have found that, on God's path, I frequently am in unfamiliar territory. I see signs that loom large, and I cannot fathom how that route will get me to the appointed destination. Sometimes, He takes a different and less-direct route than I would have chosen.

Consider the Israelites after their exodus from Egypt and the rule of Pharoah. It was a relatively short trip to

Canaan. They had a few bodies of water to cross, and God handled those crossings quite efficiently. But if we put those aside into the category of miracles for which there is no explanation, we see that Canaan was only roughly an 11-day trip and no more than 250 miles. But the circuitous route in which God led the Israelites in a cloud by day and a pillar of fire by night took 40 years.

Talk about sand in your shoes! Holy moly! Had the Isaraelites known that many people would spend their final days in the desert, they might not have chosen freedom. We know from the Biblical account that they had many lessons to learn.

For one thing, they were unhappy about the menu. They didn't like change and balked at it often. They reverted to idol worship while waiting for Moses to come down from Mount Sinai to hear from God on *their* behalf. They partied to their detriment, choosing to dig themselves into a mess.

It is my tendency and maybe yours to say,"For crying out loud… the Israelites were spared from the angel of death, delivered out of Egypt by God, chased by Egyptian chariots and crossed the Red Sea on dry land… and they couldn't just wait for Moses?" I've thought those thoughts many times. If I had the cloud and pillar as my street signs, I would have been confident in God's ability to get me the rest of the way. But don't we do the same things? Don't we have the same impatience and wayward thoughts as the Isaraelites did? I have to admit that I, all too frequently, dip my toe or my leg into the "pool of disobedience" even when I've known better. I am a slow learner sometimes. Even after lessons learned, sand storms, and grit in our teeth, we fail. After many a gritty sandwich, we still take wrong turns along the way.

GOING HOME

After a successful shopping trip to downtown Los Angeles, I was ready to go home. I wasn't comfortable because my plan was to reverse the directions and get where I wanted to be. However, it turned out that reversing the directions was not an easy task. In fact, I was in Long Beach, well past the correct interchange opportunity, before I realized I had missed an interchange. My intent was to apply what I had learned on the way there and just go home. It didn't work out that way. And it doesn't always work out that way in our lives either.

So many times, I have thought I knew where I was going, but years later, I still had not arrived. And in those times of uncertainty, which I'm sure I share with some of my readers, my relationship with God is the place to which I run. Many times, I've barely escaped situations because I've held onto the hem of His garment. In every lesson, every season, every success, and every failure, He is there. He makes lemonade from our sour decisions and turns our mourning into dancing. He is patient. He is kind. He is longsuffering. I count on that, and you can, too. Mark Batterson writes,

> If you are in Christ, you are no longer defined by what you've done wrong. You are defined by what Christ has done right. Your mistakes may define your past, but they don't have to define your present. And they

certainly don't have to define your future. If
you are breathing, it means that God isn't
finished with you yet.[1]

What is your desire? Is it working in an organizational
setting? Is it being a leader or a good parent? Whatever
your situation is and no matter where life leads you, it all
begins with becoming who you are in Christ. Whether
fulfilling the Great Commission, loving your neighbor, or
rearing your children, it all begins with you. You can't give
what you don't have.

Servanthood requires a turning from self. It requires
putting others first and having those you lead be the focus
of your leadership. The required servant heart is cultivated
through relationship, a willingness to die to self and trust
God to fill the empty spaces with more of Himself.
Servanthood requires a pliable heart that God can reshape
and remold into something beautiful. In the process, He
will create a heart that loves, a heart that endures, and a
heart that remains steadfast in godly principles.

CHANGE

When we have a servant's heart, we can touch others in
unexpected ways, ways in which individuals, churches,
and organizations can experience God. Servant leadership
will change business dynamics, organizational culture, and
our families if we are willing to follow Him. God's love
changes people. We are vessels for change.

I am unique. From my fingerprints to the way my
third toe bends over where it shouldn't, I am different. You
are unique as well. Maybe you don't have a wayward toe,
but you are a child of the King and an arrow in His quiver.

He is our Abba. Each of us can rest in that. It is not always easy, and rarely do the lessons come without pain. Sand is abrasive for a reason. It knocks off the rough edges and polishes us into beautiful treasures for His glory.

My relationships with God and all the people in my life are unique as well. Every one of them matters. Through God's refining process, I am becoming more like Him. I will strive to make every bump count because relationships matter. Will you?

---

[1] Batterson, Mark, 2011.

www.ingramcontent.com/pod-product-compliance
Lightning Source LLC
LaVergne TN
LVHW091258080426
835510LV00007B/316